From Ragamuffins . . .
. . . to Royalty:

The Private Diaries of an Edwardian Nurse

* * * * *

Tony Shephard S.B.St J.
Editor: Jenny Money

authorHOUSE®

AuthorHouse™
1663 Liberty Drive
Bloomington, IN 47403
www.authorhouse.com
Phone: 1-800-839-8640

© 2012 Tony Shephard S.B.St J. All Rights Reserved.

No part of this book may be reproduced, stored in a retrieval system,
or transmitted by any means without the written permission of the author.

Published by AuthorHouse 05/09/2012

ISBN: 978-1-4678-9715-0 (sc)
ISBN: 978-1-4678-9716-7 (e)

Any people depicted in stock imagery provided by Thinkstock are models,
and such images are being used for illustrative purposes only.
Certain stock imagery © Thinkstock.

This book is printed on acid-free paper.

Because of the dynamic nature of the Internet, any web addresses or links contained in this book may have changed
since publication and may no longer be valid. The views expressed in this work are solely those of the author and do
not necessarily reflect the views of the publisher, and the publisher hereby disclaims any responsibility for them.

Editor: Jenny Money

In January 1991 a friend of mine, Susan Lower, who works for Roy Butler at the Wallis and Wallis Auction Galleries in Lewes, contacted me to tell me about some journals coming up in their next auction. The journals in question were those of Nurse Wilby Hart (ex-London Hospital). Susan knew I would be interested in these items as she was aware of my private collection of Royal memorabilia and of my background and family history in the East End of London, and in particular the Whitechapel area. It is my pleasure now to publish these journals in book form, to be sold at, and in aid of, the **Royal London Hospital Museum, Whitechapel** and the **Museum of the Order of St John at St John Gate, Clerkenwell**. I hope reading Nurse Wilby Hart's journals will bring you as much enjoyment as they have given me.

Tony Shephard S.B. St J.

This book is dedicated to my family,
the **Hiltons** and the **Shephards**,
of Whitechapel/Bethnal Green and Hackney,
and to the following—all heroes and heroines!

H.R.H. Prince Richard of Gloucester: Grand Prior of the Most Venerable Order of the Hospital of St John of Jerusalem

Nelson Mandela: Knight of St John (1996); became Bailiff Grand Cross of the Order of St John, 23 November 2004

Phyllida Stewart-Roberts CVO, OBE, D.St J: President of Lewes Victoria Hospital; J.P Inner London 1980-95; Member of the Florence Nightingale Foundation; Dame of St John 1993; Lord Lieutenant of East Sussex 2000-08

Eva C.E. Luckës: Matron of the London Hospital 1880-1919. Created A Lady of Grace in the Venerable Order of St John of Jerusalem in 1913. Created a Commander of the order of the British Empire in 1917

Florence Nightingale: Appointed a Dame of Grace in the Venerable Order of St John of Jerusalem

Edith Cavell: 'Heroine of the First World War'; trained at the London Hospital and subsequently became Matron of the first training school in Brussels, Belgium. On the outbreak of the First World War, she became involved in helping wounded British soldiers to escape back to their lines. Sadly Edith Cavell was arrested and finally executed on 12 October 1915.

Wilby Irvine Hart

born 31 August 1881 in Bombay, India; died 1967

Wilby Irvine Hart (Bee) entered the Preliminary Training School of the London Hospital and transferred to the Hospital in 1904. She was 22 years of age, and had previously worked as a hygiene mistress. Matron's report of her is quite short; she describes her as being a good nurse and hopes that she will do her best. Nurse Hart held a number of posts within the Hospital and undertook midwifery training before becoming a member of the private nursing staff, where she went on to nurse members of the Royal Family. She was awarded her certificate on 24 October 1908.

In 1917 His Majesty King George V conferred the Royal Victorian Medal upon Nurse Hart 'For Nursing Services to H.R.H. Prince Albert' (later to become the Duke of York and King George VI).

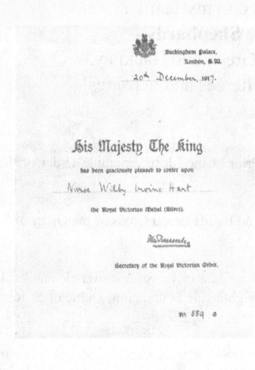

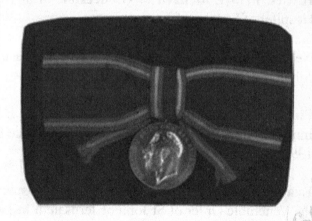

York Cottage,
Sandringham,
Norfolk.

December 25th 1917.

Dear Nurse,

Thank you and Nurse Lee very much for your letter and the knife which I received this morning. I am getting on very well down here only the weather is beastly and cold and I can't get out. It may get better later. Many thanks again to you both for all you did for me when I was ill.

Yours sincerely

Albert

Letter from Albert, future Duke of York, and future King George VI,
thanking Nurse Wilby Hart himself

Signed photograph of Their Royal Highnesses the Princess Victoria, Queen Alexandra and The Dowager Empress of Russia, Marie, given to Nurse Wilby Hart by Queen Alexandra to thank her for her services to the Royal Family.

After retiring to Eastbourne, she suffered from a stroke. At first she worked as a stone mason; later, when she was physically unfit to work with stone, she continued as a wood carver or sculptcr. Some of her work has been exhibited in the Towner Art Gallery, Eastbourne. There is a water colour of her scrambling over the rubble at Eastbourne after the bombing of Marks and Spencers in 1941. Wilby Hart also collected Staffordshire China. A niece commented 'She had a wonderful sense of humour and was a much-loved Aunt and Great Aunt'.

Acknowledgements

This book would not have seen the light of day had it not been for the help of a number of people, who deserve my most heartfelt thanks: Jane Gully (ex-London Hospital Museum staff), Dr Naluwembe Binaisa, and Jonathan Glennister, who spent hours, indeed days, laboriously typing up the transcript of the diaries; Susan Lower and Roy Butler from Wallis and Wallis in Lewes, who notified me of the diaries' existence, Roger Parish—a *scanneur extraordinaire*!—and Jonathan Evans, Trust Archivist at Barts and the London NHS Trust, the Royal London Hospital Archives and Museum, who was a mine of information and incredibly supportive of my wish to produce this book so that, long after I and Nurse Wilby Hart are gone, the Order of St John and the London Hospital Museum may continue to benefit. Finally, I must acknowledge the invaluable contribution of Jenny Money, who spent countless hours editing the text and preparing the book for publication!

Editor's Note

In editing these notebooks, I have tried to retain the original spelling and punctuation where possible. However, as these diaries were often written up after a busy day on the ward, there are the inevitable mistakes, which sometimes obfuscate the meaning—here, I have used 'editorial licence' and corrected them! There are also one or two words or expressions which we would find politically incorrect nowadays. I have chosen to leave them *in situ* and would assure readers that no offence is or was meant by them.

I would also like to thank Elaine Johnson, Kathy Lorenzo and Jerzy Rendon of *AuthorHouse* for their invaluable editorial advice, help and encouragement!

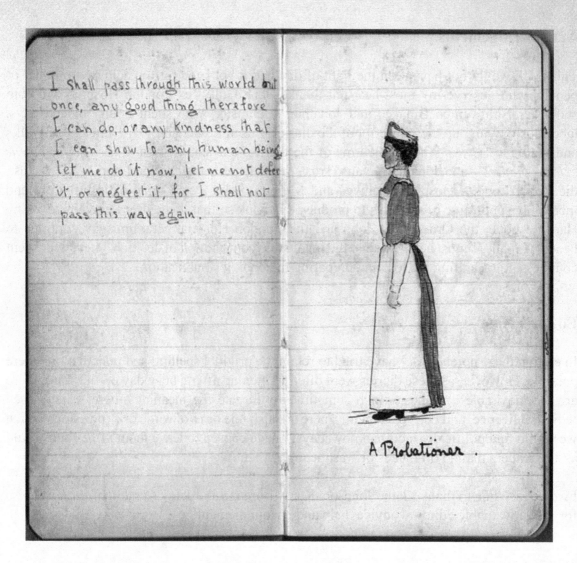

A Probationer.

I shall pass through this world once, any good thing therefore I can do or any kindness that I can show to any human being, let me do it now, let me not defer it, or neglect it, for I shall not pass this way again.

[Ed.'s note: Etienne de Grellet du Mabillier, often wrongly attributed to Mahatma Gandhi]

THE BEGINNING

Seraphs, Nursing and Otherwise

It was settled. I was to go to be a nurse. 'Where?' was the question. Interviews with Matrons are some amusing, some alarming and some dull, but the one I have most reason to remember was in some ways both amusing and alarming.

The proceedings began when one entered a room, apparently filled with desks and white capped and aproned beings, ordinarily known as Sisters, each trying to outdo the others in smile and hurry.

One's name and business being enquired into, one was requested to sit down and wait. 'Matron is busy just at present but she will see you in a few minutes'. 'But I had an appointment for 2.15 p.m. with her'. 'Matron is engaged'. One's training begins at once, but this is necessary!

Presently (a most alarming occurrence). A door at one's elbow, unnoticed before, suddenly flings itself open, with surprising force, and a Sister springs up from behind a desk, paper in hand, and enters. A moment later she returns, smiling. 'Miss A., Matron will see you'. Miss A. enters by the door which seems possessed! She tries to shut it behind her, but it will not 'come to'. When at last she does shut it, it is only to find that it springs open again and the Sister has to come to the rescue. 'Leave the door thank you, I am going out'. She goes and the door shuts—it evidently knows its mistress!

The 'Office'

The time passes very slowly in that busy room, lined with cupboards and filled with desks.

When one has studied all the Sisters, their dress and general appearance, given them characters and family histories, also all the other 'candidates' who are waiting their turns, and read all the notices on the board facing one, some of which may be of interest to those concerned, but not to the 'candidate', e.g. 'Sister's Late List', Wardmaids ditto, Operation and Convalescent Home lists, the Preacher next Sunday and 'Matron requests that Sisters and Nurses of Wards etc., etc.', one's patience and self-possession are nearly worn out and one is in a fearfully nervous condition. One is at last ushered into the Matron's august presence.

The Matron

Straight in front of the door is Matron's desk, covered with papers and vases of flowers and, behind these, Matron herself!

Who, having once seen, shall ever forget! When she presents her hand there is an uncomfortable feeling that a low curtsey and a kiss on the finger tips would be the most correct method of dealing with this plump and beringed article, but pride forbids, and a handshake is all that is ever resorted to. After the interview, one is taken for a walk through some of the wards and then one returns to see the doctor.

The Doctor

He is a strange, old, man with a shock of long, grey hair and nervous, restless hands and eyes, with a very worried expression. He makes one perch on one leg like a stalk without shoes or stockings, then stretch out one's hands and wag one's fingers like some strange game in an infant school. And finally after inspecting one's chest and teeth as if one was a horse of doubtful age, he produces a small object from his pocket and waves it before one's eyes exclaiming 'Look at this wherever it goes', backwards, forwards, up and down, behind one's head and back into his pocket. 'That will do thank you, good afternoon'.

One clutches a small, red wrapper round one's shoulders, seizes a slipper, large enough for 2, in one hand and hurries out, limping with one bare foot and a very shamefaced expression into the 'Office' where the next victim is ready and waiting.

A "candiddte" having seen the doctor —

The smiling Sister says you may dress again and, when you are ready, comes to say 'Good afternoon, this way out please, the Dr has passed you, you will receive patterns of the uniform and hear from Matron shortly'.

The Training Home

The Preliminary Training Home is some distance from the Hospital and still further from any formerly known station, so one arrives in a cab on a dull Saturday evening about 5 p.m.

The Sister in Charge

The Sister in Charge greets one coldly and one is shown upstairs to unpack and put on one's new uniform, a mystery of complicated strings, studs, buttons, collar, cuffs etc. When this is done one descends to the classroom, where the Sister is again to be seen. She presents one with a semi-circular bit of starched linen and a very neat looking nurses' cap and one is instructed how to convert the one into the other, and then put it on. The next thing one is taught is how to tie reef knots and clove hitches, both of which seem a great mystery to some people.

5

My Stable and Stable Companion

Soon after I had been shown my room, a large place with a wooden partition down the middle, another would-be nurse was brought up; she was to occupy the other half of my room. She was a nice, bright looking girl, but looked dreadfully tired and frightened. This was 'Nurse Treanor' and she had come all the way from the West of Ireland and had lost her luggage somewhere on the way. It was the first time she had ever left home, and she wished that she never had; so I comforted her as best I could and lent her some clothes which unfortunately did not fit very well, as I was some inches taller than she was, besides being larger round too; but still it was 'uniform' and nothing else mattered much and we went down together.

Our Occupations

The training home, to anybody with a sense of humour, is a most amusing place; to those without, terrible! Nobody who comes there is supposed to be less than 23, yet we were all treated as if we were 2 or 3, but never 2 and 3 together. We were taught to sweep, dust, polish taps, clean baths and basins, make beds and lay the table—which took a deal of teaching for some of us—and attended lectures on anatomy, physiology, hygiene and nursing, then came back and the Sister held classes to tell what the lecturer had meant! and what to put down in our notebooks! We were taught bandaging, 1ˢᵗ aid and invalid cookery and had to pass exams: at the end of 6 weeks. All these thing we took great pains to learn at the time no doubt, but how long we remembered them was quite another matter.

Hospital X Commandments

But all these were as nothing in importance compared with the Hospital Commandments, which were instilled into our receptive minds all the time we stayed there, but more especially on Sunday afternoons when we were all collected in the classroom and another Sister from the Hospital came and talked to us as if we were in Sunday School. Some samples of these commandments may be useful.

I   Thou shalt love no other home but me (the Hospital).

II   Thou shalt not look forward to thy 'day off' with joy or wish for thy 'time off' to suit thy convenience, but shalt serve thy Hospital without grudging, even if thine own friend and relations lie sick and thy time off be not long enough to go and see them in.

III   Thou shalt not complain of thy Hospital nor grumble among yourselves.

IV   13 days shalt thou labour and do all that thou has to do but the 14th is thy 'day off'; in it thou shalt do no manner of work, but shalt be in by 10 p.m.

V   Honour thy Chairman and thy Matron that thy days may be long in the Hospital to which thou hast come.

VI   Thou shalt do no flirting.

VII Thou shalt not become engaged to a 'Houseman'.

VIII Thou shalt not waste Hospital property.

IX   Thou shalt 'report' thy neighbour.

X   Thou shalt not *say* that thou covetest one special ward or post or position. If thou dost thou shalt not get it.

And the rest in like manner, one's duty to various people—Matron, Sisters, Doctors, Nurses and finally oneself.

One is instructed in all these matters for about 6 weeks and then there are examinations to see if one is fit to come up to Hospital, or if one had better go home.

Thursday was the day for packing one's box. Every Thursday the Sister-in-Charge goes up to see Matron and every Thursday evening somebody has an interview with the Sister, packs her box and goes home. Some Thursdays it is more than one and soon it becomes a matter of speculation as to whose turn it will be next. Sometimes there is quite a little excitement on Wednesday and even 6d. bets on the subject.

Hospital

In hospital things are very different, one feels almost like a lost lamb for a time, one misses the continual supervision, as one's day is not so regularly mapped out. One has plenty to do, but when one has real sick people to deal with one has to fit in one's work with regard to their wants, to a certain extent, as they cannot be expected to need attention *only* at stated intervals or when it is convenient for nurse to leave her cleaning and polishing.

The Arrival

I arrived in Hospital with about 21 other probationers on a Friday afternoon [6 February 1904]. We were shown our rooms and told to unpack and then to come down and have tea in the dining-room. In the dining-room, 'Home' Sister was waiting for us with a goodly supply of tea, bread and butter and cake, of which we partook, then we were each given 3 books.

1. *Black*, which we were to treasure as we would our souls, or if we thought we had none, then our lives. Their use would be explained on the last day of the month.* Inside on the front cover was the accompanying printed notice:

   *Probationer . . .

   No.   Page.

   Each probationer is required to get her book *accurately* filled up by the Sister under whom she has been working. If the Probationer has been acting as 'Special', the nature of the case must be stated; also whether the Probationer has been on day or night duty. All dates must be correctly entered. This book must be delivered at Matron's Office *before 5 p.m. on the last day of every month.* Any failure to present the book *Punctually* will be recorded in the Register as evidence of carelessness on the part of the Probationer.

2. *Red*, washing and . . .

3. *Mottled*, leave of absence, in which the Sister of the ward we worked in would enter the length of time we spent out of doors each day.

We were then told our numbers and warned not to forget where we slept. Most of us had already forgotten the numbers of our rooms, which did not correspond with our own numbers, so we had to run back to find out, which might have been a difficult business if it had not been for the help our boxes gave us, standing outside our doors, waiting for 'George' to take them away to the boxroom. When we were all collected again, we were divided into 2 parties and were conducted through the wards, our companies getting smaller and smaller as we went, as one if not more of us were dropped on each floor that we visited. I happened to be the last to be left.

* * * * *

Sister 'going round' with the houseman.

My 1st Ward (Women's Surgical)

The ward where I found myself at last was a women's surgical one and always very busy. When I got there, I was introduced to the Sister and Nurses and then left. My recollections are not very clear as to what did or did not happen that evening, but I know it was bath night and I was sent into the bathroom to give a tub to a very large and very dirty woman, who had had her nose damaged and looked a most repulsive sight. All the other patients had to be bathed in bed, as they were too ill to get up, mostly having had operations fairly recently.

I was a month in that ward under a Sister supposed to be noted for the extraordinary epithets she applied to her nurses. 'A d-lazy devil' was said to be quite mild, but she was always quite nice to me, only saying that I was 'All right when' I 'once got under way', but I was 'too much like an overfed trout' as I 'took a long time to turn round'. At the end of the month I was very loath to go from that ward to take the place of one of 'my own set' in a women's medical ward.

My 2nd Ward (Women's Medical)

I questioned the nurse who was leaving the medical ward as to what it was like. 'Oh, it is an awful place—the Sister is noted for being a perfect beast, and nothing one does is ever right. I am sorry for you', etc. This was not a cheerful introduction to my new ward, but there was no choice, I had to go. As things turned out, it was not so very bad after all. Sister left me entirely alone till one day when I was just back from dinner, when she came up to me looking like a thunder cloud and I said to myself 'Now your last hour has come'.

'Nurse Wilby Hart, how dare you try to set the London Hospital on fire?' she exclaimed in awful tones. 'I am very sorry, Sister, but I have not been trying to do so. No doubt I would have succeeded better than I seem to have done if I had tried'. 'Well if you did not try, you very nearly did so without trying. I found the towel behind the steriliser actually burning! You should never leave it like that when you light it'.

'I am sorry, Sister, if it was my fault, but I have neither lighted [*sic*] nor even been near the steriliser all the morning, so I am afraid it must have been somebody else. Shall I clear away the mess and relight the steriliser?'. 'No, you are not responsible for it. Go on dusting the lobby'. And we were quite good friends after that and she taught me a great many useful things before I left.

My 1st Night Duty

After that there were many wards and many strange people, until at last the time came when I had to 'go on night'. To anybody who has never done so before, this is a most strange experience. The 1st day I was kept on duty in the morning and told not to come back after dinner, but to go straight to bed. I went to my room and started to undress, but when about half way through, was seized with an absolutely uncontrollable desire to laugh, which I did so immoderately that one my neighbours came in to see what was the matter.

That was a very long afternoon and evening that I spent, tossing about in bed, longing to be out or anywhere but where I was, and you can't think what a joy it was to see Home Sister, who slipped into my room about 4.30 [p.m.] with a cup of tea, because she said she was sure I would not sleep the first afternoon. About dusk I began to doze a little and by the time the maids came round to call us at 8 o'clock I had actually gone to sleep!

Going to bed by daylight reminds one so forcibly of the days when one was a naughty little girl and was sent to bed early! And it takes some time to get entirely accustomed to the performance.

My 1st Ward on Night (Men's Medical)

My 1st ward on night was a men's medical, and anyone who has nursed in a 'men's medical' on night, knows its joys and sorrows. The dim light, the strange shadows and odd sounds, all add to the weirdness of being awake when other people are asleep. The least little thing makes one jump and scurry off to see what so and so is doing.

The Alcoholic Pneumonias

The 'alcoholic pneumonias' are always an added joy and terror at night. We had one in this ward who was like a lamb all day, but when the night came on, and all the other patients were quiet, he began to wake up. He demanded his clothes, so that he could go home, his pipe, matches, boots, in fact everything he could not have, and when he found you did not give them to him he threatened to get up and fetch them himself. 'Now, Sally, you just hurry up and fetch them trousers of mine. I left 'em in the kitchen'. 'I am sorry, "dad", I can't find them. I have hunted everywhere—you had better wait till morning, then we will be able to see better'. 'No, Sally, I *won't* wait till morning, that means me being late to work. You take that candle and go and fetch 'em 'ere to me, or I'll come me self with a poker, and then you'll be sorry'. 'All right, "dad", you just wait while I go'. 'Sally! hurry up can't you? I want a smoke before I go'. 'All right, when I have found your pipe'. 'There ain't no matches in this pocket nor baccy, you'll 'ave to go to the shop for some, then I'll be dressed when you get back'. 'It's no good going to the shop now; it's shut this time of night, but if you keep quiet and wait until morning, I'll get them then' and so on till either he drops off to sleep or gets so violent and noisy that he has to have a sleeping draught or injection to quieten him. With one patient there was one threat and one only that ever quieted him and that was 'I'll wash you if you'r [sic] not quiet and don't go to sleep'!

One night, my friend the 'alcoholic pneumonia' got so troublesome that the Houseman, i.e. the resident physician, had to be sent for. When he came, he ordered a sleeping draught, but nothing would persuade our friend to drink it, even when the Doctor sat on the bed and pretended to have some too and [said] that he was treating him to a drink! He was then given an injection, which only seemed to make him more lively. At last, after trying everything else, the Doctor said all he could do was to have the shackles sent over and we must fasten him up, just to prevent his getting out of bed and fighting us. So they were sent over to us, but the question was how to get them on, for the patient was kicking and struggling and spitting in all directions and every attempt to restrain him only made him so much the worse.

There was no help for it, plain speaking would not do; cunning had to be resorted to. I promised to get his boots and put them on, so that he could go home, and took the opportunity, while I was pretending to do that, to slip the shackles over his ankles and fasten them to the end of the bed—then there were his hands! This was no easy matter but, at the suggestion that I would get him some nice warm gloves, and that no gentleman ever went out without them, he submitted, but was very much surprised to find how heavy his boots and gloves were and how difficult to move.

Another patient in the same ward was ordered pills 3 times a day and when I first went, I thought how very careless the day nurses must be as they always seemed to upset the bottle, but I soon discovered it was not so. There were always exactly 3 pills on the floor and they were just close to that special bed, so I mentioned the fact and the patient was in future made to drink some very nasty mixture instead of those pills and nurse watched him drink it.

The Children

I was not long in this ward, however, and my next was a Children's Surgical, where I stayed until the end of my night duty. The children were dears, all of them, but there really is very little time to spare for play, even on night duty, with 2 nurses and 21 little people all under 7 to be washed, fed and have the bottoms of their beds made between 4 a.m. and 7, besides counting linen, combing hair and sundry other little odds and ends.

Frank, Aged 6, Feels His Responsibilities

On night, on going on duty, I heard a small boy of 6 sobbing; he had only come in that afternoon and I asked one of the day nurses if she knew what was the matter. It did not sound like the usual cry of the first day, 'I want to go 'ome'. So when I had cut the bread and butter and scalded and sweetened the milk, and one or two other little jobs that I always had to do at once when I came on duty, I went to see if I could find out a better reason than the one the day nurse had given me, which was simply that he was naughty and cross! Poor Frank, for some time he would do nothing but sob, but by degrees I discovered the reason of his woe. It was that he did not know who would fetch the bread for mother in the morning. He was the eldest of the family and the others were too little to run errands, so I suggested that Father might fetch it—no, he went to work too early—well then, Mother—no, she had just got a new baby and could not go out. Then I said I was sure one of the neighbours would do it—didn't he know of any kind person who lived near who would help Mother now he was away? He thought he could remember one or two, so cheered up and went to sleep.

Rosa, the Jew Girl [sic]

Another little thing I was very fond of, who was also said to be 'naughty and cross', was a little Jew girl of about 4. She had very bad ophthalmia in both eyes and could not speak a word of English, and so found it very difficult to know what people wanted when they spoke to her. The other night nurse never even went near her, for fear of carrying the infection to one or two other eye cases we had in the ward, so Rosa very soon got to know me and, by degrees, I taught her a few English words then, whenever she heard my voice or step, she used to feel her way to the end of the cot and there stand up and dance about calling out 'Nurse, nurse, good Rosa!' until I came to her. I know sometimes I must have hurt her dreadfully when I irrigated and dressed her eyes but, after the first time or two, I never had any trouble with her. She used to just lie still, rolled up in her blanket, and wait till it was over and then all she asked was to be taken out of bed and nursed for 2 or 3 minutes. One night, just as I was preparing to do her eyes, the Houseman came in. Rosa had put herself down in the right position and I had not troubled to role [*sic*] her up tight in her blanket, as if I expected a fight, and seeing this I suppose, the Houseman offered to hold the child while I did it. No sooner did she hear a man's voice than she started to scream and kick and fight and I had quite a business to make her understand that I would not let anyone touch her but me. When peace was restored, I did the dressing and the Houseman, who had retired into the background and kept quiet, was very much astonished at the way she submitted.

There were a great many other most fascinating people in that ward, but I always seemed to like the ones other people called naughty or ugly the best. The ones they called pretty so soon got spoilt.

Rosa, the Jew girl.

The Out-Patient Department

Soon after 'coming on day', I was sent to work in 'Out-Patients'. The work there is very different from the wards of course, but still there is a great deal to learn, if one only keeps one's eyes and ears open, in spite of what one of my predecessors told me—'that she considered it 3 months wasted from a nursing point of view' and she had 'learned nothing'. If one could learn nothing else, it offers wonderful opportunities for the study of human nature, which is never a waste of time from a nursing or any other point of view.

The Sweeper

To begin with there is the sweeper, a dear old lady who wanders round with a broom, occasionally removing some rubbish but more often 'resting a while', to offer one friendly advice or tell one a little bit of gossip. I had not been down in Out-Patients long before she discovered me—I was in one of the waiting rooms polishing a leather screen, after the patients had left, when she came in. 'Ah! you're the new probationer down here are you? Well, you

take my advice and don't you rub them screens too hard with your head down there'. 'Why not Mrs. Sargent? I have to put my head down or I could not reach the bottom; they are too heavy to turn upside down'. 'Well, I wouldn't, I know, that's all. You see the last nurse that was here in your place, she did it and went clean off her head and had to be sent home before her time and all through rubbing them screens say I'. And off she went, shaking her head.

Another day, I was brushing the 'reds' that the patients have round their shoulders, with carbolic, in the hopes of removing the livestock, which so often gets left behind by the wearers, when in came Mrs. Sargent again. 'Why you do keep doing that I can't think! In the old days in old Out-Patients the nurses never did it; you keep making work for yourselves you do! In old Out-Patients I used to put them things away and then just a shake, like this, was enough and I must say I used not to get so many fleas then as I do now'. 'Why, Mrs. Sargent, I do believe you liked the old Out-Patients better than this!'. 'That I did, in old Out-Patients the floors were all boards, with cracks between where the fleas could get and hide; here when I come along sweeping there's not the littlest bit of a hole for them to get to so they have to come hopping up my legs instead, poor things'.

One day, I came upon her sweeping vigorously and pretending not to see me, when suddenly she stopped short with an exclamation of pain. 'What is the matter Mrs. Sargent?', I asked. "Oh, it's only me potatoe [*sic*]'. 'Your potato?'. 'Yes, me potatoe for me rhumitis. Haven't you never heard of that?'. 'Never, what is it?'. 'Well, you get one and see—I've got one sewn into the hem of my gown and when it's weared away then me rhumitis will be cured. Oh, but may be you couldn't do it, because you see you have to steal the potatoe first'.

The Clinical Assistant

One's fellow nurses, Sister and doctors, are all interesting in their own way. The doctor I had most to do with at first was a young man known familiarly among his friends as 'Teddy'. I was told by another nurse that she did not like him; he was not 'interested in people'. By people, I imagine she must have meant herself, as I found no lack of interest on his part in his patients. He was a keen naturalist, of humans as well as beast and birds, and had a wonderful knack of discovering frauds and malingerers. After having taught me most of my duties as 'Medical O.P. Pro', he departed. He said he was sick of the Hebrew and, in spite of being offered a very good appointment in the Hospital, he went and buried himself in a small, out of the way station in the 'Far East'. He told me before leaving that in this way he hoped to avoid the Hebrew and to have 'ample opportunities of studying the ape'! A very good exchange he considered.

15

A Nurse

About this time, to Mrs. Sargent's great delight, one of our Probationers, having got into some small scrape over her work, found her supply of courage not sufficient to enable her to face the guns and she fled. Another proof that polishing screens was not good for the head!

Another Nurse

There was yet another nurse who came to grief over those screens. It was her turn to polish them that day and I left her at it, while I went into another room for something. Suddenly, I heard a tremendous crash and ran in to see what had happened. The screen was lying on the floor, but no nurse was to be seen. Suddenly, the screen became animated, began to heave and then I heard a stifled laugh from underneath it. When we had both somewhat recovered from our amusement, I managed to extricate her. She had propped the thing against a bench and then had started to rub the bottom, not noticing that it was gradually sliding away as she pushed it. Finally it collapsed and luckily there was no damage done, even to the screen.

Aural O.P.s

Two days a week I was on duty in 'Aural Out-Patients', i.e. ears, noses and throats were examined in a large consulting room with darkened windows and rows of tables, but I was chiefly occupied in the theatre. Here tonsils and adenoids were removed and other small operations performed. On busy days we used to get through as many as 30 cases between about 9.30 a.m. and 12.

The Surgeon

Our Chief Surgeon was a funny little man who looked like a cross between 'Dan Leno' and the 'Mad Hatter'. He wore an enormous white coat, which reached nearly to his heels, and usually stuffed a towel in each pocket with the ends sticking out, then going to the sink to wash he could find no towel on the slab and would begin to call 'Sister! Sister, where is the Sister?'. A nurse who knew his ways would then go and gently extract a towel from out of his pockets and hand it to him or, if this was impossible, would quietly remark 'The *towel* is in your pocket, Sir' and he would be satisfied.

The Surgeon.

Again, just before he began to operate, there would generally be an outcry. 'Sister, Sister, Sister! Where is the Sister?'. 'Is there anything I can get for you, Sir?'. 'No, you would not know what I meant. Sister I want the [then came a name purely of his own invention] forceps'. Of course, at first one did not know what he meant, but one soon found out and fetched them whatever they were, and again he was satisfied and his little neat white hands were a real pleasure to watch when he was operating.

The Porters

Hospital porters are very great people in all departments, but nowhere greater than in Aural Out-Patients. The patient apparently thinks they know nearly, if not quite as much, as the doctors themselves. 'Say! Doctor says I'm to put the drops in her ears. How do you do it?', says an anxious mother to a porter and he tells her. 'But say! Mister, how many do yer put in?'. The porter inspects the prescription with a sage expression and finding it says nothing about quantities, announces solemnly 'Four or five, Misus [sic]' and off she goes quite content. Or again she may question the porter on the subject of diet for her baby and will get instructions.

17

a. Hall Porter

The patients are far too numerous and interesting for me to attempt any discription [*sic*]; suffice it that I say they are of all sorts and sizes, kinds and colours, mostly dirty, but not often drunk.

Second Night Duty

After about 3 months in Out-Patients, I returned to the wards and then went on night duty again. Strangely enough, I returned almost at once to my first ward 'on night', where my friend the alcoholic pneumonia was, and found not himself, but his brother, in very much the same condition as he had been in, but it was not my fate to be left anywhere for long together this time. I found myself in a fresh place nearly every night, but mostly in the 'Isolation block'. I wandered from place to place, 'taking nights off', that is to say, taking the place of people who were having their nights off duty. Diphtheria, Anthrax, Cellulitis, Erysipalas, Cerebrospinal-Meningitis were among the cases I had to deal with at this time.

Special on Anthrax

One night, I was sent to a ward 'on special duty', that is to say, I was to be responsible for one patient only. When I got there, I saw quite a crowd round one bed, the Sister, Staff Nurse,

Probationer and male attendant, all apparently struggling violently to keep one patient in bed.

When the Sister saw me, she called out to me 'Are you the special? Come along then, this is your patient. The rest of you can clear off, just put a screen round this bed will you?'. And in about 3 minutes I found myself alone behind that screen with my patient—a huge man and strong. He had anthrax, which had been operated on. He also had had a tracheotomy performed, he coughed perpetually and I had to do my best to keep him in bed, while I cleaned the tube and dodged anything that came up through it or his mouth meanwhile, which was no easy matter, as he had no control over his movements, which were very like those in tetanus, a convulsive arching of the body backwards and forwards. The Staff Nurse never so much as came to see if all was well behind my screen, until Night Sister came and said she must relieve me while I got some food, and once she sent the 'Pro' to clear away some dirty dressings as I could not leave the side of the bed.

Why is it that one Night Nurse can always manage, by herself, the things that it takes 2, if not 3 or 4, of exactly the same kind of people to do on day?

Diphtheria Nurses

After that, I had a comparatively quiet time, nursing 2 nurses with diphtheria, in spite of the fact that one of them more than once tore the gathers out of my sleeves and apron in her efforts to get her breath when she woke suddenly.

First Staff Duty

When my 2 nurses were sufficiently convalescent to be able to dispense with a Night Nurse, I was sent to take the place of a Staff Nurse who was ill, in a Men's Surgical Ward. It was in the days before the 'Reformation' when Probationers did the sink room in the middle of the night, and there were no 'Pro Staffs' in the surgical wards. Also in this special ward any 'emergency operations' that were done returned to the ward, instead of being sent to the Junior Surgeon's beds, for the simple reason that he had, at that time, had none allotted to him.

When I came on duty, the Staff Nurse looked me up and down and then said 'Have you ever taken Staff Duty before?'. 'No, only nights off'. 'Well, I am sorry for you—we are really roudy [sic] just now, as we have been 'taking in heavily' and we don't leave off until the day after tomorrow and we are "lodging out" 6, but you have 2 beds, in case you need them in the night, and Vidal says she can take another if you are really hard up in the night. She will tell you anything you want to know, only she is going for a holiday in a day or two. She is the Staff in the next ward you know'.

All this time the most strange sounds had been coming from the far corner of the ward and the Probationer seemed to be in some difficulty with one of the patients. I suggested that I might go and see what was the matter. 'Oh no, it is all right, it is only [No.] 16, he came in with a fracture, "tib and fib" or "Potts", I am not sure which, but he was so drunk that we could not wash him, so Sister said he would have to wait till morning; that will be a nice little job for you. He has his leg between sandbags, when he can be got to keep it there. He is pushed up against the wall, has 2 bedtables over him and 3 chairs to keep them in placc. I hope he will be all right'.

A Report

'No. 17 is so and so. No. 18 on feeds, 2 and 1 were done yesterday. No. 19 is all right. No. 20, you will have to look out for him; he was an appendix 3 days ago, but he won't keep still and I am sure he has been getting someone to give him something he ought not to have to eat. No. 21 is only a fracture, but he is dying of D.T.s, nothing else, you can't trust him for a minute. No. 22 and No. 32, both 'emergencys' [sic], done this afternoon and bad. You can start dram feeds as soon as the vomiting stops, but don't increase too fast. No. 24 is on feeds. No. 25 was an 'intestinal obstruction', but he won't do; he started a very suspicious vomit today, and he is so restless and has such flatulence, and Mr . . . . says he is to have soda water, which only makes it worse. No. 26, nothing special. No. 27 is only just in and is being washed. No. 28, Oh, I forgot, 26 and 28 are empty for the night, the 6 lodgers will all come back at breakfast time—they know their way. And whatever you do, don't let Nurse forget to go and call the maids at 5.30 [a.m.]. Your Probationer always has to do it, the key is hanging on the noticeboard; she knows'.

And this was only half, I still had 15 more patients to hear about. I went through to the other division to hear what the Nurse in Charge there had to say about her patients. The result was a report very like the foregoing, there being one patient, in a splint, who was as likely as not to take it off and hit anyone over the head with it, if he was displeased, as he was to lie quiet and behave himself. 'Merely bad tempered', nurse told me.

There was one patient not likely to live through the night; another, the Surgeon was on his way to see, who might be ordered up to the theatre. Then there were 2 or 3 others, all of which [sic] needed watching carefully. The House Surgeon had just been round and left orders on 5 boards marked 'Stature', each of which it would take a good 20 minutes to carry out, and there were only 2 nurses to do it, now that the day nurses were off duty. How was it to be done? Away went the day nurses to supper and bed and soon after away went the Sister, and I was left with my one Probationer.

There was no chance of a quiet night for nurses and patients—there was my drunk man in the one corner, kicking his bedtables, waving his broken leg in the air and throwing the sandbags on the floor, the other at the far end with D.T.s, keeping up a perpetual running commentary on all that was going on, and a great deal that was not, and trying to get out of bed; the man that 'would not do' calling every five minutes or so for a drink and in the intervals vomiting all he got, and almost every other patient in the ward asking for something. This was all very well to begin with, when the 'Pro' was in the other division.

The Surgeon came and decided it was not necessary to operate on the new patient that night, so we were let off that extra work, but we had plenty without that. I found after a time that, if I called out to my drunken fracture, 'Oh, daddy, mind your leg, put it down or you'll hurt it', when I saw it flourishing in the air, he would do what was required of him much more quickly than if I went to him and tried to put it straight without, and as there was such a noise already, a little extra did not make much difference and saved a lot of running and no little danger of making a compound fracture out of a simple one, so I simply 'kept my eye down the ward' when I was busy at the other end and, as soon as I saw an upheaval beginning, I called out and the upheaval subsided, and I could go down at my leisure and see that the leg was in a good position. By morning, I found it quite unnecessary even to shout to him to put his leg down, as he took on that job himself, and I kept on hearing the remark 'Oh, daddy, mind yer leg' coming from his bed and strangely enough he obeyed himself quite meekly!

About 1 a.m. the Probationer came to say she had finished what she was doing, might she go and get our meal ready, and off she went, while I was left to 'keep an eye done [sic]' both wards at once. Hardly had she gone to the scullery when I heard the door open into her division and a step in the ward. I went through to find Night Sister looking very serious. 'Where is your Probationer, nurse?'. 'In the scullery, Sister'. We went round that side and, just as Sister was going on to the further ward, she said 'Now, nurse, remember this division must not be left on any account. Matron would be very grieved if she knew there was no nurse in the ward when there are patients in this condition'—and she went. Luckily, when she returned 10 minutes later to go down the other side, the Probationer had returned and we were one in each division.

With many interruptions, we managed to eat our meal—one in each division still—and struggle on, until it was time for the Probationer to go and do her share of the sink room, while I was again left in charge of the two sides. As luck would have it, I was in the side that the Probationer generally looked after when Sister turned up again, this time in my division first, and I went through to her. She greeted me at once.

"Never leave this side for a minute"

'My dear nurse! How could you leave this division? It is perfect madness, you must never leave this side for a minute'. 'I am sorry, Sister, but one of the men in the other division wanted something and I had to go to him'. 'Where is the Probationer?'. 'In the sink room, Sister'. 'Well, that does not matter—you must not leave this division on any account'.

Needless to say, I was ready to meet her when she returned down the other side and she did not think of asking me if the Probationer was in the side I had just left—but it was hardly necessary; you could still hear the clatter in the sink room going on. Morning came without anything very dreadful having happened and we did not forget to call the maids.

A Staff Nurse.

The Trials of Having 'An Extra'

Two nights later, when we had settled down considerably, I was sent an extra nurse to help. 'And now', said Night Sister triumphantly, 'you will have no excuse for leaving the ward with nobody in it' and so also I thought till I tried. I left the 'extra' in one side while I went through to where my own Probationer was cleaning the 'brights' and settled down at Sister's table to write the orders for dressings, stimulants and several other little odds and ends that fell to the Night Nurse in the division of labour. No sooner was I comfortably settled than our 'extra' walked in and set to work beside the Probationer. I asked why she had left the other side. 'Oh, I could not find anything to do in there'. So I said I would do my ordering in there and took my books through after telling them that they were on no account both to leave that division at once, one of them must stay in if the other went out. Hardly was I well started again before my 'extra' wandered in again. 'We have finished the "brights", what shall I do now?'. I gave her something I thought would keep her quiet for at least half an hour and went on with what I was doing.

A few minutes later, I heard a man calling in the other division and asked my 'extra' what the 'Pro' was doing. Was she busy, as the man seemed to be calling in vain? 'Oh, she went into the scullery some time ago. Shall I go and see what the man wants?'. 'No, you stay here and go on with what you are doing. I will go in there, and mind you don't leave this place until I come back'. So, off I went again. When the Probationer came back to the ward, I went into the lobby to cut dressings and fill the tins, ready to go and be sterilised next morning, but I had only been out at it a very short time when, behold! my 'extra'. 'Can I help you do that?' she said, 'the "Pro" says she will put round the sugar and butter pots and fill the tins in both divisions'. 'Nurse, when will you understand that you must not leave the ward? Go back and stay in whichever side the "pro" is *not* in. I will find something for you to do in there. You must not come out'. And so we continued the whole night long. I found it far harder work to divide my 3 people between the two divisions than I had ever found it to split myself in two and turn up in whichever division Night Sister appeared.

The Ways of a House Surgeon

The laziest person in the whole of the Hospital in those days was 'the beautiful boy with the violet eyes', and he happened to be our House Surgeon. Not that he went to bed early—we only wished he would—but he got up so late that his morning round either extended far into the afternoon, or else got left out altogether, and his evening one usually began about midnight. He never did a dressing or P.F.O. if he could get out of it, nor took the trouble to make his Dressers. The consequence was that he was always having to be sent for at most inconvenient moments, to himself, and for this, took his revenge by ordering the most inconvenient thing he could think of at the moment, subsiding into a chair and watching our struggles without the least effort to help.

"The Beautiful Boy with Violate Eyes"

One night a boy, who had had an operation not long before, was very bad and seemed to me to be getting steadily worse as the night went on. 'The beautiful boy etc.' had not done his evening round, although by that time it was next morning, so I sent the Probationer to Night Sister. She came and looked at the boy and decided that 'the Houseman had better know'. So off she went to find him. Presently he arrived, sauntered up to the bed, looked at the boy and then announced his intention of 'transfusing' him. The most usual form of transfusion in use in the wards at that time was 'continuous'; in fact I had never seen any other, except once, during an anaesthetic, when the 'continuous' was out of the question. So I sent the Probationer off up to the 'Surgery Beadle' for the apparatus and saline, and set to work erecting footstool, bath and other necessaries on the bed table, saw that there was a kettle boiling and remade the bed in the correct style.

When I announced the fact that all was ready, 'the beautiful boy' looked up languidly at the carefully erected contrivance on the bed table and said, 'What's that?'. I told him. 'Oh, I did not mean that; I always do "intravenous"—you might get the things for that'. So all my erection had to come down and be hurriedly removed and the new things found. I hunted high and low and found a syringe here, a measure glass there, a bit of tubing somewhere else, but only old and bent needles. The instruments, of course, were all right, but nothing else seemed to be in order. At last, I thought I had everything but the needles and told him so, suggesting that we might manage with one from the 'continuous' at a pinch. 'The beautiful boy' looked up again from his chair in front of the fire. 'I have all my own things for that. Sister always keeps them for me, they are all together in a box in the medicine cupboard'. Why he had not told me that at first was a mystery; instead he preferred to waste both his time and mine, quite unnecessarily, for there at the top of the medicine cupboard, in a neat little case, was everything that was needed. The performance over, he retired to bed and we cleared up the mess. The next time he was sent for, he selected [sic] to give a stomach wash to the unfortunate patient (not the same one). It generally was either a stomach wash or transfusion, usually the later [sic].

Day Duty

My next move was to 'come on day' and I went for a short time to a Women's Surgical Ward as 'special' to a gastric operation case and took the Visiting Surgeon, whom I had never seen before, and who walked into the ward hat in hand, as a rather respectable and nice looking patient's relation, very much to his amusement. But it enraged Sister immensely.

My 1st 'Pro Staff' Ward on Day

I only stayed there for a few days, however, and then was sent to be 'Pro Staff' of a small ward, which was the offshoot of a larger one, but separated from it by 2 doors and a short bit of passage, while my sink room was much further away across the passage. When I first went there, the cases were distinctly dull. I had 8 beds, which were nearly always filled by old fractures, or the most unpresentable and uninteresting of the operation cases from the parent ward.

After I had been there a short time, there was a re-allotment of beds and all my 8 fell to the share of a Surgeon, who had previously trained and got his certificates as a navigator and was commonly called 'the Skipper'. He was as outspoken and bluff as any sailor and the thing that annoyed him more than anything else was for a nurse to be nervous in his presence or not to know anything he asked about. If there was any hesitation in answering questions, or any show of fright, poor nurse's fate was sealed. She was bullied and shouted at, and even sworn at, at the least provocation, but if nurse stood boldly up and answered or even cheeked him, it was quite another story; peace and good will reigned as long as she remained in the ward.

The patients were nominally men, but I was very seldom without one or more small boys, one of which [sic], a little chap of about 6, had a 'separated epiphysis' and also very bad pemphligus, and every movement was so painful that the poor little fellow used to scream out. One day his mother was in the ward when I had to move him and, instead of his usual scream 'I hate you', he swore as vigorously as anyone I had ever heard. His mother pretended to be very shocked, exclaiming 'Oh, Frankie, 'ow can yer? Where did yer get all that? I can't think'. Whereat the youngster, still almost crying, shouted back at her 'Garn! Yer learned it me yerself, yer know yer did'.

Another patient I had was an old man who had had a fractured pelvis and, when he was getting better, the hardest work I had was to prevent him from doing all the work of the ward. When he was still flat on his back, he used to get any of the other patients who were up to fetch him all the red jackets or shirts I had to mend, the minute I was out of the way, and start on them himself, and he sewed extremely well, even in that position. But when he was up I hardly ever dared leave the ward for a minute, as I never knew what he would be doing when I got back: sweeping, dusting, washing up, all came alike to him, but the one thing he could not do for himself was to get into bed and the first day he tried it was a hopeless failure and his astonishment and embarrassment were enormous when I came up quietly behind him and lifted him bodily in!

For a long time after he went out, he always used to turn up on theatre days—because he knew I would be busy, and he was not well enough to start regular work—to see what he could do to help and often, on coming down late from the theatre with an operation case, I would find him taking entire charge, giving the patients their tea, or later taking the basins round for washing, or even getting my tea ready for me if I had had none.

One evening, when our own Sister was away for her holiday, one of the porters brought a case up for me. He was most apologetic, as he said he did not like leaving the man with me, as I was alone, but there was not another vacant bed and the man was too drunk to send home, so in he had to come. He was just capable of walking and talking in his own peculiar way and was, comparatively speaking, quite well, but had come up to have his glands operated on, on the following day.

When I suggested that he should undress and get to bed, his reply was merely 'Oa no! Baint a goin' te shtop 'ere!'. So I said that surely since he had come he would stay and see the doctor and sister. 'Well, shyay jus' lil wile te pleash yer'. 'But won't you get into bed—you will be so tired sitting up there? I'll help you'. 'Tell yer I, I'm bl . . . . I ain't agoing te get te bed sho there!'. 'All right, you sit in the chair by the fire till Sister comes'. 'Sh, shant shit by the fire, goin' 'ome. Goo bye, sho pleashed te a sheen yer'. 'Well, you don't seem very pleased, since you won't stay any longer. Come with me and we will walk round and look at the patients, do you know any of them? You were in here before, weren't you? When you had your tongue done?'. And so I babbled on as I walked arm in arm round the ward with my very unsteady companion. When we got back to the fire I suggested that he should rest a bit, so he sat down and there was peace for about two minutes and I tried to get on with my work.

Suddenly, I saw him pick up his hat and put it on, so I made across the ward and took it off and shook hands warmly. 'So pleased you could come, "dad", make yourself at home and sit down by the fire, won't you?'. 'Shank yer sho much, but I shink I musht be goin''. 'Oh, no, not yet, it's quite early still'. But all the same he tried to put his hat on again, so I pushed him down in the chair and sat down beside him and took his hat away again, then we got up and turned round, shook hands and sat down again.

Presently we had another walk, arm in arm. By this time all the other patients had retired under the bedclothes, to try to smother their laughter. For about an hour this performance continued, at the end of which time the Sister, who was taking the regular one's place while she was away, came to do her evening round. She was very much surprised to find the patient not in bed! I was very much surprised that she found him in the ward! But I explained to her what was going on and why none of the other patients were visible, so she kindly excused me this time. Then she said that she would stay with the man while I went to the Receiving Room and fetched a porter to put him to bed. I was gone about 2 minutes, but when I got back there was Sister with her back against the door, looking very white and scared. 'Oh, I have had such a tight few minutes, Nurse, I am glad you are back'. She had been trying to be dignified and could not have played the fool to save her life.

Presently the porter came, and the 'Houseman' and between them they managed to get my friend into bed. He was given a sleeping draught and an injection to quiet him and, after a time, he went to sleep, but I did not feel at all happy about him and had to keep on going to look at him. I felt sure there was something wrong with him. I was by his bed when the Night Nurse came on duty and said I did not feel happy about him then, but he looked all right and was asleep, so I started to give my report. But about half way through I had to go and look again. This time there was a change and he had almost stopped breathing. I called to the nurse to come to him and flew into the other ward for Sister but, before she could get the 'Houseman', in fact before I went off duty, which was in less than five minutes, that man was dead. The drink by itself would not have done it, nor would the draught or the injection but all these, combined with a slightly defective heart, had proved too much for his strength.

Every Sunday afternoon I was visited by two small boys. Their names were Jack and Albert Anthony, or 'Albranthony' as he called himself. Jack always wore a blue bow and Albranthony a pink one under his chin. They had both been patients at sometime or other, but that was before I knew them. They used to turn up regularly about 3.30. First they went and had a look round the big ward, to see if any of their friends happened to be there, and saw Sister, then they came in to me and, after the first Sunday, always took it upon themselves to get my tea and lay places for 3, one on top and two underneath the table. Then they would sit themselves down on 2 hassocks and drink tea and munch bread and butter almost indefinitely. At 5 they solemnly cleared away and washed up, generally waiting after that to help get and eat the patients' next meal, which started rather after 6 on Sundays. Then they departed and I saw no more of them until the following Sunday.

Our "harmless lunatic"

Our 'Harmless Lunatic'

I suppose it was quite excusable, but I was very much puzzled at first by a rather dotty old man asking me if they were twins! Also remarking that I was young to have two such big boys! I remembered afterwards that I often called them 'Sonny', which is our usual method of addressing any male patient who is still unmarried and beardless.

The same old man once called me to him in the night, after I had changed over to night duty, to ask if I did not think it very nice and a 'satisfactory arrangement' that I and my 'dadda' should have the same sort of work in the 'same establishment'! This stumped me entirely for some time. At last it dawned on me: I had had to have a male attendant to look after this very old man for a few days after his operation, because he was so unmanageable and would tear his dressings off every time my back was turned, and he thought old Dunn, the attendant, was my father. If you only had known Dunn!

'Dunn'
He had not really got a black face only the ink ran. The rest is really like.

More of the lunatic.

'Dunn', the Male Attendant'

He was good nature itself, but impossible to keep awake at night, and absolutely terrified of a violent patient. More than once when he was sent to look after a D.T. patient in the big ward, Nurse sent him through to me to ask if he might stay and look after my quiet and harmless patients while I went to help her, as he poor man was too frightened to be of any use!

The old man who took Dunn for my father was always known as our 'harmless lunatic'. When he was able to get up, he was always striking attitudes in the most inconvenient places he could find and then looked hurt if we asked him to move. One day, while Nurse and I were sweeping in the morning, he persisted in standing exactly in front of first one and then the other of us, in his favourite dressing gown and socks. At last, Nurse got rather cross and told him, if he did not keep out of the way, he would have to go back to bed. Whereat he exclaimed in an ecstatic voice: 'Beautiful creature! Public houses have no attraction for me, all I want is to take a pretty girl (like you) down to the river and I would be happy all day long in the fields. You must come and have tea with me and I will show you my greenhouse, where my wife dries her clothes when she has a bath. I make beautiful tea! One teaspoonful of tea and five beautiful strong cups of tea. None of your hospital stuff. Come any day, my greenhouse is worth seeing'. He stopped abruptly, because he found himself suddenly being bundled into bed and he did not want to go and all the other patients were laughing at him! He was about 60 years old and awfully ugly.

An 'Employers Liability Act' Case

S . . . B . . . was even more ugly, but he was only 13 and had a squint, but I don't think I ever met a more patient and plucky boy all the time I was in hospital. Everybody noticed what a nice child he was, until the papers got hold of his story and everyone made a fuss and talked of him; then he became most abominably cheeky and self-assertive and no wonder! But that was after he left the ward and became an Out-Patient. He had been employed in some factory, where part of his duty was to help in making the twisted wire cords for electric lights. The process entailed the production of a great amount of waste naphtha and this the boy was given, by one of the men he was working with, to throw away. He was not told where to put it and so took it to the fire and, before the stuff had had time to leave his hands, it had flared up. When they brought him into hospital the whole of his right hand and arm and part of his left hand and forearm were coated in a thick layer of black India rubbery substance, which had been left when the naphtha had burnt out, and his hands and arms underneath were very severely burnt.

It was weeks before we could get all the naphtha away and months before his burns were healed and even then his hands were nearly useless and more like birds' claws than human hands; but the last time I saw S., not long before he stopped coming to Out-Patients for massage, he could grip my hand quite vigorously enough and, though I don't suppose he will ever be able to double his fists, a drawback in that walk of life no doubt, he could use his hands enough to go back to work. That must have been a full year after he left me and my ward.

After having spent almost 7 months in this one little ward, I was very much disgusted at being 'sent on day' to another ward, when I only had a fortnight left before the end of my first 2 years and my 'month', the holiday one has when one sheds forever the check frock and Probationer's aprons. I was nearly on my last legs at that time, but I just managed to hold out until the last, so at the end of my Probationer days I was able to say that I had never been 'off duty sick' for a single hour, of which I was duly proud.

Holiday Duty in a Women's Surgical Ward on Day

The ward I was sent to for my last fortnight was a Women's Surgical Ward and different from any other I had been in before. The women were rarely, if ever, content and nor was the Sister. Worry was not the word for it; she worried the patients, she worried us, but she worried herself worst of all. We were on the race from morning until night and yet we had never done what we should or, if we had done it, we had certainly done it wrong. I could not make it out, till one day Sister unwittingly threw some light on the subject. I forget what I was doing but, whatever it was, Sister came up in the middle. 'Oh, Nurse, don't do it that way, Night Nurse would never have it done like this'. It was Night Nurse! She was the terror of the whole ward, Sister included! She bullied the 'Pros' and the patients alike and Sister put up with her because she was a good manager! And she was afraid of her.

One morning I found Night Nurse in the lobby 'slanging' one of my Probationers. It was the girl's first ward and she was not accustomed to that sort of treatment and consequently, being of the meek order, had melted into tears, imagining that she had proved herself entirely incapable of ever becoming a nurse, because, forsooth, she had spilt a little water on a tray Night Nurse had just wiped! I sent her away as soon as I saw what was happening, and told Night Nurse that, in future, if she had any complaints to make about my Day Probationers, to make them to me and I would deal with them myself. I found if their wits were a little scattered when they first came into Hospital, it was infinitely better not to scare their few remaining ones entirely away, if you wanted them to do any work (there was plenty for her to do looking after her Night Probationer). This seemed to annoy her and she never lost an opportunity of complaining to me all the rest of the time I was there, but she left my Probationers alone.

A Difficult Question

One morning, on coming on duty, I enquired after a certain woman, who had had 'excision of gut' and a 'Murfey's [sic] button' inserted a few days before. She had been very bad the previous day and seemed too weak to be able to rally properly: 'too patient to get on' I said, but Night Nurse had a different idea. She had been 'very troublesome and lazy', would not 'sit up and wash herself'. At this I exclaimed 'Surely you don't let her wash herself yet, do you?'. 'Oh, she is only lazy and won't pull herself together: she could quite well if she liked; Mr . . . . said she needed rousing, so I have been trying'. Presently, as I passed the bed, I spoke to the woman and asked how she felt. 'Oh, Nurse, is that you? I can't see you today, but I am glad you day nurses are back. I am afraid I made Night Nurse awfully angry with me because I could not wash myself. I did feel that queer and I could not see to the end of the bed'. Then came a chorus from the beds around: 'Yes, and she shook her, she did'; 'I call it a shame, don't you?'. 'When a body feels that bad, too!' and so on. I cheered the woman up as best I could and pacified the others, promising myself that it would not happen again, and inwardly determined that, if Sister did not already realise what a bully her Night Nurse was, she would before I went off duty. It was all very well for her to try it on with me, or even the Probationers, but this poor helpless sick creature—it was too much!

I was on duty in the morning and called Sister's attention to the woman one or twice; her temperature was very high and her pulse rapid and Sister was anxious, but not alarmed, about her condition. I noticed, as the morning went on, her increasing restlessness, her complaint that she could not see and the unhealthy, clammy feeling of her hands. At about 11.30 I took fright and was certain there was something more wrong than was to be accounted for by mere laziness, or even shock after an operation, but I wanted something definite to tell Sister. I was tired of saying that I did not think she was looking so well, so I took her temperature—it had dropped far below normal and her pulse was thready and I could hardly count it. Here was something definite to tell Sister, but I could not find her: she had left the ward and had gone, I did not know where! When she returned it was the patient's dinner time and she would allow nothing to interfere with that, and before I could catch her after, she had gone to her room for her lunch. I was nearly frantic and went back to the woman, who seemed no better and had been quite unable to take the food set before her. Suddenly, I thought I would have another look at the dressing. I had looked several times during the morning and seen nothing, but this time there seemed to be a very suspicious bulge under the bandage and on the edge of the dressing an ugly stain. I did not wait to think of Sister's lunch any longer, nor did she wait when she heard what I had to say, but promptly sent a note to the 'Houseman', who arrived with an Assistant and 2 Dressers within ten minutes, but it was no use, the 'Murfey's [sic] button' had given way and she was dead before anything could be done.

That evening, when giving my report to Sister, I told her of what had occurred in the morning, but it seemed to make very little impression. 'Yes, Nurse, I am afraid we all make mistakes at times, Nurse is hard but she is a good nurse and a splendid manager'. I could not help exclaiming: 'Then I hope I will never be a good nurse, or a splendid manager, if one has to make oneself thoroughly hated, by bullying every one, even one's patients when they are dying!'. Sister merely smiled at my outburst and said 'Ah, Nurse, it is not *always* the best women who make the best nurses' and there we left the subject and I don't believe Night Nurse ever heard anything from Sister about the matter.

I had one or two bouts on the subject of bullying with Night Nurse before I left, because I refused to make the patients get about and help if I did not think them fit for it, and even let them get back to bed before their usual time if they were extra tired. With great disdain, she told me that I aught [sic] to go to a medical ward, surgical patients did not do so well if they were petted and pampered! She did not seem to realise that most of our women were thoroughly rundown and ill before they came in for their operation. The women never come in until they are practically at their last gasp and are usually absolute wrecks when they arrive.

An Interview with Matron and the Results

One Wednesday evening, when we were very busy and racing specially hard, because it was lecture night and the Probationers always had to go a few minutes before 8, so that they could tidy themselves and be in their places in time, the ward telephone rang and somebody came to say that 'Matron wished Nurse Wilby Hart to go down to the office at once, please'. I could not think what had happened! I did not know of anything that had gone wrong in the ward and could not imagine what Matron wanted to speak to me about. I suppose I looked worried because, as I hurried along the ward, all the women began calling to me: 'Cheer up, Nurse, you're all right'. 'We'll stand by you, never fear'. 'Send Matron up to us if she says anything nasty' etc. I was away nearly three quarters of an hour! Matron had sent for me to say she would like me to come back after my holiday as an 'Assistant' and holiday Sister'!

When I returned to the ward, a few minutes before 7, I was horror struck! There was the ward, sure enough, but in an unrecognisable condition. The ward that Sister prided herself was never out of order, was in absolute chaos! Bed tables, bedclothes, chairs, tables, patients and plants, all mixed up together in hopeless disorder. The other Sisters from other wards were wanting to get through to go to dinner and could hardly force a passage! And there, in the midst of all, was Sister! 'Nurse, what have you been doing?'. 'I haven't an idea, Sister, I have been in Matron's office for the last half hour and I don't know what has been happening'. I was too bewildered to know anything. A few mornings later, I said goodbye and departed. A nurse who was seeing me off asked if I had been up all night or if I had only seen a ghost? But I was still too bewildered to know even that!

It was 6 weeks before I returned to the Hospital, as I took this opportunity of being ill; in fact I had started the very night I got away and, at the end of a month and, in spite of a sea voyage, when I said 'Now is the time to return', my very refractory relations dared to differ from me, so far as to tell Matron I was not yet fit to come back and so, as I walked downstairs, bag in hand, and ready to start, I was presented with a telegram from Matron, saying I was to stay where I was until I was fit to work! Perhaps not quite worded that way, but implying they had no use for crocks in Hospital.

RETURN TO HOSPITAL

I arrived at the Hospital after my holiday on 23rd day of March 1906 in the evening, and was greeted by those in the office as 'Sister' though as yet I had not so much as tried on my blue frocks. One of the Assistant Matrons came to my room and told me that on the morrow I was to have breakfast in my room. Home Sister would see about it and have it sent up and then, a few minutes before 8.30, I was to go down in my outdoor uniform, so as not to attract attention, as I would be without a cap, to her room, where she would give me one, ready made up, and pin it on for me, for all the world as if I were to be crowned or anointed in secret! Then she would take me to whatever ward Matron wished me to work in at first.

A Sister.

First Day as a Sister

I did not get to sleep till late that night and, when next morning came, I was roused at about 5.30 by the bell which calls the nurses, and lay awake wishing I had never come back, till 7.30, when the maid came in, smiling, and brought me hot water! Formerly I had had to fetch it if I wanted it. She beamed on me and called me 'Sister' too, and hoped I would stay in that room, as she liked having a Sister on her floor. Why, I can't imagine, because it must mean a lot of extra work, as Sisters do not do their own rooms and have to have supper fetched on their half days off and are altogether more waited on than any 3 or 4 nurses put together.

'Home Sister' brought me up my breakfast herself and wished me good luck, saying that, if there was any way in which she could help me at any time, she would be only too willing to do so. At 8.25 I duly arrived at the Assistant Matron's room to be crowned!—or rather 'tailed' as we always called it. Then I was walked solemnly through the garden to the ward, while everyone we passed turned to stare at the 'new tails', and then ran on to tell someone else and ask 'What has *she* done?' or 'Why has Matron tailed *her*?'. Nobody ever knows, but everybody always guesses. It is the same with every new 'blue' that [*sic*] 'comes out', as it is expressed. But the nurses' curiosity is as nothing compared with that of the older Sisters; the most trying ordeal of the whole of the first day is going to dinner, but that comes nearly at the end.

Arrival in the Ward

When I arrived at my destination, it proved to be a ward where I had worked once or twice before and I knew and liked the Sister and Staff Nurse. Neither of them fussed or worried or, if they did, they never let anybody else know it and so the work went smoothly and both seemed quite pleased to see me, which is a most unusual occurrence for, as a rule, an 'Assistant' Sister is looked on with suspicion by the 'Staff' and is considered a bother by the Sister! Hardly what is intended, but still it often is so.

I was solemnly introduced, a form which is always gone through, however well one is known. 'Sister, I have brought you Miss Wilby Hart. Matron wishes her to learn all she can from you before she has to take holiday duty'. Sister expressed her pleasure and promised to do all she could and the Assistant Matron departed. First, Sister said, I had better come and she would explain all about the 'papers' while she was doing them and then she would take me round and tell me all she could about the patients. They were medical women, but the ward was not very heavy just then, which this Sister thought rather an advantage, as it would leave her all the more time to attend to me!

The 'papers' proved to be the daily and weekly 'bed returns' order forms, return of patients, Hebrew patients, 'admission tickets', Marie Celeste Samaritan Society requests for tea, butter and sugar, dangerous list, lists of probationers, 'Chaplain's list', and many others, a good many of which I already knew about, as I had been responsible for a good deal of the ordering—Sister's table and the stationery in my wards at night when a nurse—but still there was plenty to be learnt. Then we went round, counted the spoons, forks and knives, measured the stimulants for the day and inspected sinks, scullery, bath, etc. to see that all was clean and in order. Then came the patients and Sister told me all about them, not only their present condition, but their past and probable future history.

Presently she went to the Office to report; this happens daily between 10 and 11 a.m. In the meantime, I was to look after the Probationers—one was very new and very scatterbrained. She was supposed to be clearing out the rubbish from the patients' lockers, but generally managed to remove their greatest treasures and leave the rubbish! She was also to give lunch round and would, if left to herself, certainly give everything to the wrong people. The medicines she was not to be trusted with—Sister asked me to see to that myself. At dinner time I helped Sister 'serve' and then feed some of the helpless patients, after which Sister explained the mysteries of the 'diet' book and how to discover how much milk, bread and soup one may be allowed to order for a given number of patients on certain diets, and presently I went off duty.

When I came back at 4 p.m., Nurse asked me if I had made any other arrangements for tea, or if I would come and have it with her in the ward. I had made no arrangements and was very grateful for the invitation, as I had no wish for solitary confinement in my room, which would otherwise have been my fate. Then came the part of the day which I enjoyed more than any other—the 'evening work', when I was allowed to do just what I chose. I made beds, washed patients and helped with the suppers until just before 7, when Sister, who had been off duty since 5, came back and told me it was time I came to dinner and, if I was quick, she would wait for me, as she knew that it was horrid going in by oneself on the first night.

Going to Dinner

It was bad enough with an escort; we were by no means the first to arrive and all the others turned and stared as if I was some sort of strange, wild beast. How thankful I was when I was able to escape from the dining room! One of the other Sisters, whom I had known before, caught me as I left the room and asked me to come to her room until it was time to go back to the ward, and I was only too thankful to get anywhere out of sight. She fed me on coffee and biscuits, even though we had only just finished dinner, and promised me that it really was not so bad when one was used to it and the other Sisters were used to you. At 8 o'clock we returned to our wards and at 9.20 the day nurses went off duty; then, for the first time, I saw a most curious sight.

The 'Show of Hands'

Each Probationer, as she came to say 'Goodnight' to Sister, held out both hands, first showing the palms and then reversing them and presenting the backs! Sister nodded to each one in turn, saying 'All right' or 'That's better', 'Goodnight' or some such remark. I waited until the little ceremony was over and the nurses had gone then, turning to Sister, demanded an explanation. It appeared that there had been a great increase in the number of nurses going on duty with 'fingers' lately and Matron had insisted that some, at least, were due to carelessness on the nurses' part and it must be put a stop to and so those Sisters who were anxious to do their best for the Probationers under their care had instituted this little ceremony. They had a 'show of hands' every night, to see that all their probationers' hands were clean and in good condition. So many bad fingers come from chapped or cracked fingers, carelessly cleaned, or small cuts being left uncovered, or even pin pricks sometimes were enough.

Bed at Last

At 10 p.m. we went off duty and to bed. Oh! what a long day it had seemed and how I hated everything, myself particularly, for being so discontented. The only enjoyable time had been between 5 p.m. and 7 p.m., when I had been allowed to behave like an ordinary, human nurse, instead of a stuffed image. But really Sister had been very good and she tried to give me things to do, so that I should not feel quite so useless, and Nurse, too, let me do very much as I liked and did not look offended when I happened to try something that was usually her work.

The Probationers were really the worst; I don't think they would have let me lift hand or foot for myself, if they could have helped it! If I started to do anything, they would come bustling up and try to take it from me. 'Oh, Sister, can't I do that for you?' or I would have all my utensils snatched away and tidied up for me, almost before I had time to stop using them! There would be one, perhaps, crouching on the floor with her head in a cupboard, cleaning it. Somehow, she would perceive that I was coming in her direction; out she would struggle and scramble to her feet, because she had been taught at the Training Home that one should stand in the presence of a Sister. Another, with her arms full, would see me making for the door and fling down her things and hurry to open it for me and, whether or not I had intended to go out, I was bound to then. At last, in desperation, I implored them to get back into their cupboards and pick up their things and take no notice of me when I was harmlessly engaged on my own affairs. It was time enough to stampede when I came officially with instructions, or to scold them! And so they were a little better, but not much, until a fresh batch came and we had the same performance all over again.

Receiving Callers

In the following days, between 6.30 and 7 a.m., when I was still lying in my bed, I had several of my old nurse friends to see me and wish me luck. It really was nice to see them, even at that hour of the morning. One's time off as a Sister, besides being shorter, very rarely coincides with that of the nurses, at any rate of those one wants to see, so this was often the only time one could meet them, and I had no intention of entirely dropping my old friends if I could help it.

Beckey's Theological Theories

Some days later, when Sister and I came on duty, Nurse came up to us in high glee. She had a story about 'Beckey'. Beckey was a regular 'hospital baby'. She had come in when about a year old with some obstruction in her throat, which had made it necessary for her to have a trachiotomy performed. She was now 5 and had not been at home for more than 9 months of her life since she first came, for the simple reason that her parents found her quite unmanageable! She could perfectly well have gone home with her tube in, only whenever she was sent away from hospital, she flew into such a passion and screamed, till she forced her tube out and then could not breathe properly and began to turn black in the face; her parents were so terrified that they came running back with her to us!

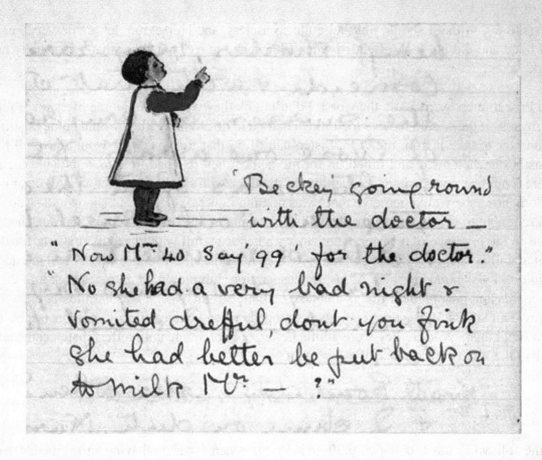

'Beckey going round with the doctor —
"Now M⁻ 40 say '99' for the doctor."
"No she had a very bad night & vomited dreffull, dont you fink she had better be put back on to milk M⁻ — ?"

It appeared from Nurse's story that Beckey's theological instruction was distinctly mixed. One of the women had died the night before, after Beckey had gone to sleep. In the morning, when she woke, she asked Night Sister what had become of Mrs. 20. 'Oh, she has gone home', Night Nurse told her as she went to the bath. 'No she ain't, she's gone to 'eaven. But who will look after her when she gets there? She's too bad to look after herself'. 'Oh, the angels, we all have angels to look after us, even you have got one you know, Beckey'. 'No I ain't', says Miss Beckey, 'God-an-Jesus looks arter me'. Poor Night Nurse felt squashed and there was silence for a little, while the bath was continued. Just as proceedings were coming to an end, Beckey began again—she had been thinking. 'I know, when God-an-Jesus is "off" then the angels is "on"', she remarked in triumph, having solved the difficulty for herself, which had been suggested by the contradictory instructions which she had received. Her ideas were entirely bounded by the Hospital and its customs. She could not even imagine a Heaven without 'on' and 'off' duty times!

Michael's Angels

One Sunday a nurse came back from church very pleased with something she had heard—not the sermon, but a little Jewish boy, Michael. He had persuaded his nurse to take him with her, not seeing why other boys who were not Jewish should be allowed to go with her, while he had to stay in his ward. He got permission from his father, as Nurse would not take him without, and then on the following Sunday appeared in church. As the choir entered, there was a shrill little squeal—'Oy, Nurse, Nurse look—*die kleine angel kinde*!' and for long after Nurse said he used to talk of the angels he had seen in the Christian Synagogue.

Mrs. Richards

One day there was a certain Mrs. Richards brought in; she had had a 'stroke' which left her partly paralysed down her left side and she could not speak very distinctly so that, here as everywhere else I had been, I was usually called upon to translate her grunts and signs into plain English. I don't know why but, ever since I had first come into hospital, people always had an idea that I could understand the incomprehensible and I used to be fetched when a patient with a more than usually peculiar dialect was brought in, to translate for Sister, Nurse or the Doctor. It did not matter what it was—French, Yorkshire, Yarmouth, Yiddish, Devonshire, Irish, drunk or baby language, or merely an incapacity for saying the right words—as one I had who could never remember how to ask for the bedpan, but used to demand all sorts of things, such as a tent, socks, soup plate or sponge in the attempt.

As a rule, one only needs a little patience to find out what they mean and to make them understand what one wants. But this is not Mrs. Richards. She, poor thing, had not been in long before she had another stroke, which rendered her absolutely helpless and inarticulate, but still she had an idea that I could understand her when the others did not and she used to start grunting in a most pitiful way whenever I went near her and sometimes certainly I used to make out, mostly by guess, what she meant. She was dreadfully thin and altered after her second stroke; one would have thought that she was at least 70, instead of only 37, which was her real age and when a few days later she died and her husband brought her little daughter of 8 up, I thought it wiser that the child should not see her, so I took her through to the lobby and told her; the father had not thought of doing so before.

Different Points of View

The child had not seen her mother since she came in, so certainly would not have recognised her, and I told her that her mother had altered and looked ever so much older, so I thought perhaps she would rather not see her now, but remember her as she had known her when she was well. To this the little girl agreed but, when I took her back to the ward, her father was furious and said I was 'depriving the child of her last privilege and pleasure'! He said she was to go and look at her mother. So we went behind the screen, but she saw nothing, as she was crying and hiding her face in my apron all the time, but the father was satisfied that the poor little thing had 'done her duty and had her pleasure and privilege'. What strange ways some people have of looking at things! I remember one mother whose chief regret, apparently, at the death of her little daughter of 14 was that 'She was just beginning to be a little useful now'. But the majority are not like this; their affections are very real and cannot be gauged by the amount of use their children are to them.

39

The Inventory

Once every year there is an inventory in every ward and O! what a business it is—every sheet, every blanket, every everything not in use at the moment has to be arranged in the lobby, with its name, number and date showing, on a certain day. The linen on the beds has to be arranged so that the corners of the sheets, blankets, draw-sheets, pillows, pillowcases and nightshirts are showing, with the name of the ward, number and dates on them, and woe be to anybody who disarranges those corners before the inspection has taken place.

For days beforehand, no linen belonging to the ward may be used or sent to the wash, anything that is likely to get soiled has to be borrowed from another ward, so that nothing shall be missing on the great day. All the instruments, crockery, glass, water pillows, mackintoshes, bedrests, everything has to be counted and, if not visible, accounted for. Somebody is sure to drop and break a tray full of things, or manage to secrete shirts, towels or pillowcases, just before the event—then there are heart-rending scenes. If it is crockery or glass, somebody is sent flying over to Shepherds—the shop where the Hospital crockery is bought. Probably they are 'just out of' the particular article one wants but, if the messenger is very urgent, Mr. Shepherd will say that he will go over to the 'Hospital Store Keeper', who sent for the last lot yesterday, and borrow them back from him, so as to be able to sell them to Sister, as she needs them so very badly! If it is linen of any sort, one flies round the ward hunting and asking everyone about it. Somebody is sent to the laundry, another to the linen room, flock pillow room, anywhere that anyone can think of; probably a nurse from the next ward brings whatever it was back a little later, having removed it by mistake!

Men's Medical

When I left this ward, I was sent to a Men's Medical. I had worked here before also, but under a different Sister and, though I had met the present one two or three times, I did not know her well, but she was a most charming person when one did know her.

The Sister

The sort of person that everybody turns to, if they are in trouble or need advice, but she was naturally so reserved and quiet that, unless one came in contact with her a good deal, one hardly realised that she existed.

Two Staff Nurses

The two Staff Nurses were a really funny contrast and were always at daggers drawn—I used to think sometimes that they would even have come to blows if it had not been for Sister's pacific [sic] influence.

No. 1: The one, a prim, little, person with a very pedantic way of speaking and an absolute certainty that she was always right and must, therefore, never forget to hold her own against the onslaught of her less fortunate and far-seeing fellow Staff, who, of course, was always wrong as they never agreed on any subject.

No. 2: The other, a very hot tempered, energetic, little Irish woman, who said and did exactly what she thought she would. Her language was not always Parlamentary [*sic*] though forcible, and one knew she meant what she said, which was not always the case with the other.

Sister and I both agreed that No. 1 was the better-trained nurse, but No. 2 was far and away the more desirable of them to live with. One always knew where to 'have her'. No. 1 had a marvellous capacity for eluding inconvenient questions when they were asked by inquisitive Sisters. No. 2., when she caught her at it, would tell her plainly that it was 'as good as a lie'. But, all things considered, we had wonderful peace in that ward.

Spring Cleaning

While I was in this ward, we had what is known as the 'Spring Clean'. It may come at any time of year, as some part of the Hospital is almost always being done. The performance takes place every year; that I suppose is why it is a 'Spring' clean . . .

First of all, the patients and their beds are all packed into one division and screens drawn across the openings. Any beds that are *not* occupied are stripped—the mattresses sent to be fumigated and the frames sent down to the yard to be overhauled—then, while the men are rewashing the ceilings and painting and the women washing the walls and scrubbing the floors, we take the furniture, chairs, tables, lockers, electric lights, glass lotion and dressing jars. Everything that can go in the bath goes there and is scrubbed, then brought out, dried and polished, no matter what it is. The smaller things are done in basins and the ones too big for the bath have a good wash down on the floor. The whole place swims in soap, water and furniture polish. Sister and I found the tails of our caps dreadfully in the way when scrubbing the legs of armchairs or the bottoms of lockers and so took to standing the things on the lobby tables. We tried pinning our tails to our backs, but then we couldn't bend or turn our heads, so that was no use.

It takes several days as a rule for a ward to be thoroughly cleaned, if there is much painting to be done. Then, of course, there are the Sisters' rooms and the lobby, which all have their turn. Nearly every afternoon, when I was well in it with a dirty apron, no sleeves and up to my elbows in soapsuds, the telephone would ring.

Taking Visitors Round

'Will Miss Wilby Hart please come to Matron's office at once to take visitors round', and off I had to go to clean and tidy myself as best I could and hurry down to the office. This nearly always happened just as we were about to have tea, if it had not done so before. In those days, we generally had a sort of picnic tea in the lobby, or the half of the ward that was being cleaned, as there was no room to spare where the patients were. We all had it together, nurses and Sisters, and we used to have great fun over it too, so that I did not appreciate having to go—one dreadful day I tramped the Hospital with batch after batch of visitors, each more uninteresting than the last, from just after 2 till past 6 p.m!

One company I took round—I think they were Americans—tried hard the whole time to be intelligent and questioned me about everything they saw. On our way round Out-Patients, we happened to pass a room used for examining eyes; there were no windows and the walls were pained black. I opened the door, just to let them look in, and immediately I heard a voice at my back: 'Oh, this must be the "Light Treatment", isn't it the Light treatment, Sister?'. I replied that it was not—it was merely a 'dark room'.

An Italian

Another time, I was sent for to take an Italian gentleman round. It was supposed that I could make him understand, but he spoke *no* English and I had *no* Italian, but we discovered that we each knew a few words of French. He begged not to be taken to see anything horrible; he was very tender-hearted and could not bear to see people suffer. So I took him to a men's ward, where I knew that they were mostly convalescent and in very good spirits. But I had hardly got him inside the door before he made off, almost at a trot, to the other end, where he waited for me, looking neither to right nor left. He explained that he could not bear to see people in bed! So I thought Out-Patients would be the place for us, so off we went. I tried to get him to look at the great crowded waiting hall, but he would not. I took him to the 'Light Department', but had the greatest difficulty to induce him to come in and, when I at last succeeded, he raced to the other end and stood with his nose almost flattened on the further door, till I came and let him out. I was beginning to wonder why he had come. He was not interested in the drugs in the Dispensary, or the pill making, so I tried X-rays. I showed him the 'screen' and tried to explain what he would see when the light was put out, and then we went through the usual performance of looking at the bones in my hand and the nails in the electrician's boot and a few other things but, when the lights were turned on again, he was sitting with his back to us and had seen nothing! This was too much! I took him to the front door and directed him to the nearest tea shop, where he could get some refreshment before he started home. It was all I could do for him.

The Hebrews

One set of wards that nearly always interests visitors are the Hebrew ones. For a long time, a certain number of beds have been kept specially for Hebrew patients but in 1904 four large wards were opened entirely for them. There they have a kitchen of their own, with a very strict Hebrew cook, so that everything can be done 'according to the Law' in that department.

It is very puzzling at first when one goes to work there, because one must always remember that milk must not be mixed with meat, i.e. milk must not be put in a feeder that has ever had beef tea in it, even if the feeder is washed between. The milk puddings provided for the patients are given them at 11 a.m., whereas the meat part of their diet does not come on until noon; because of the law which forbids the mixing of milk and meat, they are even kept at different meals. Even butter may not mix with meat, so must never be used for frying meat, fish or vegetables. Suet and dripping may not be used in the making of puddings or cakes which will be eaten at teatime, but they use different kinds of vegetable oils in cooking. I was explaining one day how we had two sets of crockery and knives and forks, on account of this, when a patient chimed in saying that, of course, they had different knives for meat and butter because, if they did not and used one knife for both, it would be made into a Christian and could never be used for anything again! Another thing they are supposed to be very particular about is always to wash before meals which, no doubt, is a very good rule but, when it degenerates into spitting on either hand and then rubbing the two together, as I have seen done, it is almost as well to disregard this law.

The nurses in these wards, whether Jewish or Christians, were supposed to, more or less, observe the Sabbath and refrain from needlework, or anything else unnecessary in the ward, between the setting of the sun on Friday and the same time on Saturday, because it seemed to upset some of the stricter Jews so much to see the nurses going on as usual, even though they were Christians and kept their own Sabbath the next day!

Lighting the Sabbath Candles

The little ceremony of candle lighting is rather pretty. At Sundown on Friday a clean, white tablecloth is spread on one of the tables, all the men cover their heads and candles are taken to the oldest man in the ward, who lights them and prays over them, then they are set on the table and may not be moved or blown out, but must be kept just as they are, until they burn out of themselves.

Passover Cakes

Upon the first day of each Feast of the Passover, a large Passover cake is hung in each ward and is not removed until a new one replaces it the following year; these cakes, and the phylacteries in little glass cases on the doorposts, are nearly always of great interest to people going over the Hospital. They are surprised that we 'give in to the Jews so much', even going as far as to allow such an unhygienic thing as a cake to be kept hanging in the ward for a whole year!

The Ward Maid—Mrs. Love

But I must return to the ward I was working in and confess to a great omission: the Ward Maid. She reigned supreme in the scullery and imagined she did in other places as well. If one was in her good books, one was happy; if not, one's life was not worth living. She did her work splendidly and everything she had to do with was spotless but her temper, which was not always under the best of control, could be terrible! If she did not like one, nothing could ever be right, but if one got into her good books to start with, she would do anything she could—and that was often no small amount—to help, and one would be allowed a far greater amount of liberty in the scullery than those who had failed to win her approval.

How I Won Her Favour

I had won her favour, quite unconsciously, the first time I went to work up there, by bearding her in her den, rather than the then Staff Nurse, who absolutely terrified me. I wanted to be enlightened on some subject and chose her, rather than the Staff, as I thought 'Mrs. Love' the lesser of the two evils. In consequence, in later days, when I was pressed for time, or was short of nurses, she would come and do all sorts of little odd jobs which were not her work at all, but mine—but there were certain things the bravest might not do and one was to touch the fire in the ward or lobby. One day she and the ward maid from the next ward were discovered fighting with their brooms because 'Emma' had put some rubbish on Mrs. Love's fire, after she had been asked not to do so.

Mrs Love   Mrs Taylor
                Emma

44

Just about two days before I left this ward, a little boy was brought in to us with pneumonia—he was about 2 and a half years old, but could not go to the Children's Ward, because he was said to have Whooping Cough as well. He was very ill and cried almost continually, poor little Teddy: nurse told him that, when he was better, he should go home. So every time anybody came near him he wailed 'I's be 'ere', hoping that he would be sent home. Later, when the desire to go home was less, the cry was kept up in the vain hope that, if he was better, Nurse would not come and put a poultice on, wash him, or give him his medicine, but all to no purpose. If Nurse meant to come, come she would, no matter how well he was.

The nose & Teddy, 1st appearance

The Nose and Teddy: First Appearance

He was not an attractive sight in those days: his nose, which was never one of his strong points, was very red and swollen; in fact he seemed nearly all nose—but I knew him better later on and so will say no more of him now.

Back to the Women's Surgical

From here I returned to the ward where I had been when I left for my month. 'Night Nurse' had now changed over and had become 'Day Nurse'. She still ruled with a rod of iron but what a difference there was in her manner to me! I had been a mere 'Pro' then, but now! 'Butter' was not in it, but I knew it was only my blue frock and tails that made the difference. However, she never let me see her bully the 'Pros' or the patients. It probably went on just the same when I was not there, but at any rate they had a respite while I was about. My time in the ward was very fully occupied, as Sister's one idea was to make me do and see as much as I possibly could in the time.

My Duties

When I came on duty in the morning, after the preliminary of listening to reports from the Night Nurses and going round, Sister would ask me to begin the dressings, as she wanted them done early. The 'Dressers' never came till later on and she objected to their doing anything if she could manage to stop them. Doing them all round in both divisions, I could very rarely finish until after 11.30. Then Sister would say 'I think you had better go off duty now, Sister, and if you will come back in time to get the patients ready for the theatre I would be glad. The first one goes up at 2 punctually'. One is supposed to have two full hours off duty and half an hour for lunch, but it did not occur to Sister that it was impossible to get 2 and a half hours between about 11.45 and 2 p.m., as well as get from 3 to 5 patients ready!

In the afternoon there would sometimes be as many as 5 cases to be operated upon and these would keep one up in the theatre till well on in the evening, then down we came and rushed through the evening work until 7 p.m., when one had to go to dinner. Dinner over, there would be linen to put away, ribbon gauze to fold, bandages to wind, binders to make and messages to run, which kept one going until bedtime. Sometimes one would be sent for to the Office, just as one was going off duty, then one took visitors round till lunchtime, bolted one's lunch and came back to the ward. One's off duty time then would have to be put off till after dinner, from 8 to 10 p.m., and one generally crawled straight into bed, as by that time of day one does not want to go out. On the days when neither surgeon was operating—we had 2 in that ward—one or other was sure to be holding a class on one or more patients in the ward.

The Visiting Surgeon's Clinical Lectures

Oh, there was such a fuss; every patient had to have her hair redone and fresh ribbon put on and a clean, white jacket. Those who were to be lectured upon had clean sheets; all manner of weird lamps and strange instruments were produced and arranged on a table—they were never used for anything—and absolute silence was enjoined on everybody in both divisions of the ward. It might have been some kind of God, or at least the whole Royal Family, that was coming, instead of one man who did the very same thing at least once a week.

'Scrubbing'

My first experience of being, on my own, as a 'Scrubbing Sister'—that is, the one who looks after the 'Scrubbers' and does all the odd jobs that have to be done between 9 p.m. and 10 a.m. or thereabouts. One is supplied with a pass key and one ranges over the whole of the Hospital and one's duties are many and varied.

Serving Room and Registers

First, at 8.50 p.m., one goes to the nurses 'Serving Room' to see that the maids wait properly at the Night Nurses' breakfast. Then one helps to wash up spoons, forks and glasses for the Day Nurses' supper, which starts at 9.20 in the same room, or else one marks them in the attendance register to show they were present and in time for their meal. How one's brain whirls at first when they come trooping in. Some tell one their numbers audibly, some so that one cannot distinguish what they say and some not at all. All go so quickly that, even if one knows them, one has no time to mark them present before half a dozen others have passed. Yet those registers have to be filled up, and correctly. Every nurse has to be marked for every meal and, if she is absent, found. If anyone is late six or more times in one quarter, she looses [*sic*] her next day off, so one must be accurate. Certain days in the week, instead of marking the nurses in the registers, one wanders round the corridors to see that the nurses do not talk or make a noise going on and off duty at 9.20. By the time all the nurses are either on or off duty and are out of the corridors, it is time to get the room ready for the other Night Sisters. They use the 'Physicians' and Surgeons' room to sit and have their meals in while not going round the wards.

Blotting paper, ink and pens have to be put out for them and large sheets of foolscap paper for the reports, which go to Matron in the morning. Then the meal is brought in at 10 p.m. We all sit down to a strange repast. It is more like 'high tea' than anything else. At 10.30 p.m. I and my key used to depart to unlock the doors, so that the scrubbers could get into the offices, telephone rooms, dispensary and all the other places that have to be cleaned by night.

The Scrubbers

At 10.45 p.m. the scrubbers begin arriving. Such a funny crew! All over 45, mostly widows, and not a few more or less decrepit. Some are old, worn-out ward maids who are too old and stiff for day work; others have scrubbed ever since the beginning, when scrubbing was first invented! They could tell one wonderful stories that, if one believed them, would make one's very straightest hairs curl. They all turn up by about 11 p.m. and go down to a certain cupboard where their pails, mops, dusters, floor cloths and bowls are kept. When this is unlocked one has to keep a sharp lookout to see that none of these old ladies make off with some other old ladies' belongings. They always squabble over which pail is which and who certain rags belong to. Then one goes to another cupboard and doles out soft soap, washing powder, pynka sticks, soda, and when necessary, new rags for dusters, new scrubbing brushes, mops, brooms, flannel for floor cloths, and little odds and ends.

If one or more of the scrubbers think fit to stay away, as they do sometimes, one goes up to the front hall to see if there is anybody waiting about who will do to take their place. If not, their share of the work has to be divided among the others. I had heard that it was a very difficult task to get the others to do more than their usual amount, but I always found that, if I asked them to help, as a personal favour, they all clamoured to do it and the real difficulty was to prevent them from all fighting for the largest share!

47

The great thing in looking after these old dames is for them never to know when to expect one to turn up, or which direction one will come from next, then they are afraid to get up to too much mischief. If they know when to expect one, they can arrange accordingly and do nearly anything, from going to sleep to stealing the pens and blotting paper out of the offices, or the drugs from the dispensary, or making love to the night porters.

At 1 o'clock all the scrubbers collected in the 'Receiving Room', while I presided over the milk can; they each came armed with a mug or small jug, as they were allowed half a pint of milk each night, in addition to the 2s. 0d. which was there [*sic*] portion—6d. more than the day workers, as they did not get their dinner, which the ward maids and day women all had. This money was not given to the regular ones each night but at the end of the week, but sometimes I could not resist their intreaties [*sic*] to be allowed 6d. or 1s. 0d. 'in advance' when they had had a 'bad week', which often meant that their children had been ill, or they had been helping a married son through hard times.

Mrs Norris of the "luney passage", hardly looks 45.   Mrs Williams [cleanest & most trustworthy

Some of Them

One little woman, Mrs. Norris, had a consumptive husband; she was one of the few who were not widows. He spent most of his time in the Brompton Hospital but when he did come home she always had a very bad time. He needed so much care and meant so much extra expense. She often used to come to work looking terribly sleepy and tired, as she had hardly had any rest all day, but she was always cheerful, in spite of everything. She it was who scrubbed what was known among the scrubbers as the 'luney passage'—and, if I found fault with her for making too much noise or having too many lights on, her excuse was always that she had to, to 'keep her heart up' when she was in or near the 'luney passage'. She could not do her work otherwise. This passage was a semi-circular little passage, which was a sort of branch off the main one, where the 'padded rooms' were and the small rooms where noisy patients were put, when they could not be kept in the wards, for fear of disturbing the other patients too much—and hence its name.

Mrs. Williams was a dear little mouse-like person. She was by far the cleanest and most trustworthy of them all. I never had to tell her that her water was too dirty and she must change it. I only once found her asleep and then she was on her hands and knees, her scrubbing brush in her hand and her head in the pail! She was slower over her work than the others, but very thorough.

Mrs. Norman could never hit the happy medium in her work; she had a good deal of stair work and either forgot to use her scrubbing brush at all, and just slopped the water about, or else thumped the wood of her brush so hard against the wall and stairs that she used to wake the patients in the wards near by.

Mrs. Gray was by far the oldest of them all and thought herself quite at the top of the tree. No one might take liberties with her! She did what she chose to call 'mostly dry work'. She used to clean the Secretary's room and offices, where there was more sweeping and polishing than scrubbing to be done.

Mrs Norman one of my Scrubbers.

Mrs Gray, doing her 'dry work' –

Mr Schaffe

Mrs Aitkin

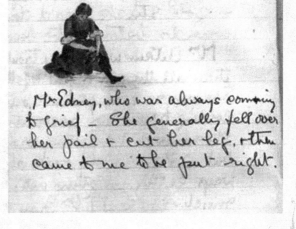

Mrs Edney, who was always coming
to grief – She generally fell over
her pail & cut her leg, & then
came to me to be put right.

Mrs. Schaffe.

Mrs. Schaffe was one of the most amusing of them; she was of German origin and looked on at her neighbours with wonder and surprise. She told me they were so dirty and lazy; they neither washed nor sewed! She 'could not understand a woman being like that!'. One night she insisted on nearly undressing to show me her own underlinen, She told me with pride that she had made all the things she had on herself and she always washed them herself too. Certainly they were beautifully done. They were made of good stuff too and with her name embroidered on each garment. She was very fat and, unluckily for her, the 'clinical theatre' fell to her share in the work. Here there were fixed benches, with desks in front of them, rising tier upon tier, one above the other, and so close together that she could hardly squeeze between them. One night, as I went my rounds, I heard most unusual sounds of merriment coming from this place, mixed with shouts of somebody imploring for help. I hurried in to see whatever she was up to and there she was, gasping and laughing, having slipped and got stuck, head downwards, between two benches.

Mrs. Aitkin was more trouble than all the others put together. She was so very plausible and, according to her own accounts, she never did anything wrong, but Oh, she was sly and was always getting the others into mischief. She and Mrs. Cray were the heads of rival parties and would not so much as eat their meal in the same room, so Mrs. Cray and her party, when they had got their milk and made their tea, retired to the Secretary's office. Mrs. Aitkin and her party went to the Steward's office and in these retreats I left them for half an hour and never interfered, unless they became too uproarious. At 1.30 I returned and started them off with their work again, which they continued until 5.30 a.m., when work stopped, and I locked up their things, after inspecting them to see that they were properly cleaned before they went into the cupboards. Every now and then I also held an inspection of their baskets, to see that they were not making off with any Hospital property, or anything else they should not have.

It really was pathetic to see the way they raked over the dustbins to see if there was anything there they would like to take home. As a rule, if they found anything, they used to bring it up to me to ask if they might have it; such queer things they seemed to want sometimes, but flowers were what they seemed to like best; old, dead things that had been in the wards and were thrown away as being too bad even to give to the Ward Maid, and certainly too bad to be kept, were treasured by these poor old things. Mrs. Norris was specially delighted when she got some as she said 'They will do beautiful to take to me 'usband hat the Brumpton'.

After the Scrubbers went Home in the Morning

After the scrubbers had gone in the morning and I had locked up again, I went to call the maids in the furthest Home and ring the bell for the Day Nurses. At 6 a.m. I had to be back in the Physicians' and Surgeons' room to mark the Ward Maids; they all had to be in their wards by 6.30. If any of them did not turn up, again I went to the front hall to see if I could find anybody; as a rule there were 2 or 3 women there waiting to see if they could get an odd day's work but, if there were none, I had a list of names and addresses of women who would come if wanted and I would send a porter round with a note. Then came marking the Laundry Maids for breakfast and the Doctors' Maids too; these maids not only did the doctors' rooms, but dusted all the offices my old people had scrubbed, and lighted [sic] any fires that were needed—I had to see that they did it properly.

Mrs. Collier

There was one funny old woman among the day workers who was known as the 'corridor woman'. Her name was Mrs. Collier and she was very deaf, but always insisted on stopping me, in the front hall by choice, to declaim on the virtues of some thick combinations I had given her, which had been so shrunk that I could not get into them. She would tell me how well they fitted her, patting herself all over meanwhile, and talking in what was intended for a whisper, but to my thinking was nearer a shout.

Mrs Collier.

When I first started scrubbing, there were two of these very ancient ladies; the other was Mrs. McCarthy, but one day she was taken very ill, so I took her off to the 'Receiving Room' and got a doctor to see her and, instead of going to work, which she had fully intended to do, she was packed off to bed in one of the wards. About a week later, I met Mrs. Collier looking very mournful and mopping her eyes as she went along. I stopped her and asked what was the matter. 'Oh, I been to see Mrs. McCarthy an' she'll soon be gorne now, she will, she'm all a dying uppards'. 'She's doing what, did you say?' 'Dyin' uppards. Everyone dies either uppards or downards, one begins at their toes and works up and t'other begins wi' the 'ead and goes off at their toes, don't yer know'. With this lucid explanation I had to be content, as Mrs. Collier began to dust and mop her eyes alternately with the same rag, mumbling to herself: 'An' now I'll be the oldest day woman lef' and all be meself so to speak'.

Another day, when I had met her about three times, and always in places she had no business to be in, she said: 'Well, me dear, you do allers be movin' about, don't yer niver git tired o runnin' from one plice to another?'. But from this it will appear that I never did anything but attend to the cleaning of the Hospital, but it was not so; I did many other things besides.

After the first night or two I managed to get myself sufficiently into favour with the other Night Sisters to get them to let me go up to the theatre whenever there was an operation. They also told me of any interesting cases in the wards, which I used to go and see; then there were nasal and œsophogeal [sic] feeds and anæsthetics to be superintended in the wards and continuous transfusion to be started—all of which, though really the other Sisters' business,

53

were often handed over to me to do, specially by one Sister who was not a very active person and so was only too thankful to be rid of all these little extras. I, too, was very pleased to have the chance of doing and seeing a little of the actual Night Sisters' work before I had to take their nights off, as that was part of my business.

Nights Off

On Saturday nights my scrubbers never came; it was their night off, and so on that night one week I would take the place of the Sister who managed the East Wing. The next week I superintended the West Wing and the third I had a night off myself.

On Friday night I used to do one 'round' with the Sister whose place I was to take the following night and make notes of any special cases to be remembered on the next night but, even with that, it was no child's play on the Saturday night to remember everything and write an intelligent report for Matron at the end. One was responsible for some 300 odd patients—men, women and children—and in the report one had to make a note of every patient who was on special treatment, anyone whose condition changed noticeably in the night, and of course any operations, anæsthetics, new patients, deaths, births and if one had to call up any of the doctors in the night.

A doctor who has been called.

The Calling of the Doctors

This calling of the doctors was entirely in the Sisters' hands and didn't they make a fuss if they were called unnecessarily! And no wonder, poor things; often they had not gone to bed until the small hours of the morning and, if they were not down by 9.30 a.m. next day, there was no breakfast left for them! Some were very good when one went to rouse them; others it took a good ten minutes to make them realise one was in the room and another ten to make them understand what was wanted of them and which ward they were to go to. Others again appeared to wake up at once and understand but, the minute one's back was turned, went to sleep again and one had to go back and begin all over again.

The Receiving Room Bell

The most startling thing that ever happened in the night was the ringing of the 'Receiving Room bell'. In each ward there is a bell which rings down to the 'Receiving Room' and registers the name of the ward whose bell it is. It is only used when the nurses are in great difficulties and need assistance immediately. It may mean that a patient has gone off his head and is too strong for the nurses to manage by themselves; it may mean suicide or unmanageable or drunk relations, or fire, or in fact any kind of accident which must be rectified at once and which the nurses cannot grapple with by themselves.

When one heard that bell it was impossible to stand still; it makes one move, even if one does not realise at first what it is. I have heard it from the furthest corner of the Hospital—nobody waits to think if it is dignified to run. The first person to reach the recorder calls the name of the ward and everybody who is not bound to stay where he or she is makes for that ward, the quickest way they know of, some by the lifts, some by the stairs. One hears a rush of feet in the passages, the clank of the lifts, and anybody not knowing what was happening would certainly think that Sisters, Doctors, Dressers and Porters had all gone hopelessly mad if they happened to see the race. My propensity for moving, which Mrs. Collier so much disapproved of, happened to be distinctly useful one night. I had been on the wander and had heard some slight commotion in a ward overhead and so went up to see what was going on. It was an old friend of mine, a heart case, who had been in before; he was feeling rather bad, poor old thing, and was distinctly fractious and was throwing things about. He had thrown himself out of bed last time he was in, so I warned Nurse to look out and went away, as he was not really violent and there was nothing to do but watch him.

Some hours later, I was in the other wing of the Hospital on the floor below when I heard the alarm sound in the 'Receiving Room' and made off as fast I could, to find out which ward wanted help, wondering as I went if it could be this same old man. As I went I was surprised to hear the bell go again and there was no sound of feet on the stairs or in the corridor. When I got to the Receiving Room, there were all the porters standing gazing at the recorder open-mouthed and, just as I got there, the bell rang again for the third time, but no ward was indicated on the board. I told them it was no good standing like that, but that they had better first try the ward where my old man was and then if it was not there, they had better divide forces and some go up each side of the Hospital till they did find the right place.

a mischievous baby.

Then I went off myself and arrived at the ward door, just as a very frightened Probationer was hurrying out to fetch somebody, as the bell had brought nobody. I sent her back to help Nurse, who was by herself, and ran down and told the Sister whose side it was and went on to find the 'Houseman' whom I had seen busy in the Receiving Room with a new patient. He came at once and he and I got back to the ward before those porters, who had started in the lift, had made their first appearance. I suppose they did not believe in undertaking what they thought might be a wild goose chase, though they all did it a few nights later, when I was in the theatre and could not get out to see the fun. This time the bell rang violently and did register a ward, one of the children's ones, and they all flew up to find that a mischievous baby had climbed up the bars of its cot, while Nurse was busy, and had reached over and pressed the button himself. He was rather frightened, poor mite, at the result, but it taught him not to do it again.

One Saturday night, when we were having our 10 o'clock meal, one of the Assistant Matrons came in. She asked who was in charge of the West Wing that night and I answered that I was. She then proceeded to tell me of a patient who had come in for some quite slight operation. I had seen her the night before—a nervous, elderly looking woman. The operation was to have taken place that night at 8.30 and was to be the removal of a small and perfectly harmless growth; it was being done at her own request and as a matter of convenience, rather than necessity.

At 8 o'clock, when the lights were put out, she suddenly sprang out of bed and rushed out of the window on to the balcony, where she tore up and down, trying to climb the rails which, luckily, were very high. Then she flew to a window, which looked into the passage, and made faces and shook her fist at everybody who passed. It was Sister's weekend off and the nurses, after trying everything they could think of to persuade the woman to come in, without success, sent down to the Office to ask what they should do. The Assistant Matron went up to see if she could help, as sometimes the sight of a blue frock is enough to cause submission, but this time it only made matters worse. Then they sent for the Doctor, who came and tried to force her to come in, but she flew at him and tried to bite and scratch and so he gave it up. After that, they all went into the ward and left her prancing up and down in her nightgown and with bare feet, like some wild animal in a cage. Presently, one of the nurses crept out with a wheelchair, dressing gown and shoes and called her, saying that, if she would come and put these things on and sit in the chair, she would take her right away where the Doctors would not find her when they came, and so at last she was caught and taken down to the 'luney passage', but when she got there, she suddenly became suspicious and thought she was being trapped and jumped out of the chair and started running up and down the passage with a Special Nurse in attendance. There the Assistant Matron left them to their own devices. She did not think there was much likelihood of the woman going to bed, or even submitting to stay in one room, but she begged me to see that there was no chance of her escaping and getting out into the street.

The first thing I did that night was to do down and see that all was safe and that one of the outer doors had not been left open or unlocked, as I had sometimes found them; then I went to see the woman. Nurse had managed to coax her into a room by that time, but did not know how she was going to keep her there, so we thought of a plan. Nurse was to pretend she wanted to go away and leave her and I set her on to guard the door and prevent Nurse from getting out. This answered splendidly and the next time I went to see them she was sitting huddled on a chair planted against the door—she let me in, saying 'Well, my goody, you have lef' me a job! That nurse of mine is a dreadful gad-about-girl. I ain't agoin' to let 'er out at this time o' night, not me, I'll sit 'ere until mornin' afore I lets her go. There's no knowin' what she might be up to! It would not be what one might call respectable to go out now!'.

I had some difficulty in getting her to let me out, till I explained that it was my business to go round to all the rooms and see that nobody let their nurses out and, much as I would like to have stayed, I was obliged to go on, in case any of the other ladies needed help. By about 4 o'clock in the morning she had condescended to get on the bed, after making Nurse promise solemnly not to escape. There she sat, perched upon the pillow, making Nurse do her hair. She had not very much, but insisted that it should be done in as many plaits as possible, and she demanded that I should tie them all up with cotton, as Nurse was not quick enough, and, when I had finished, I never saw a more grotesque sight in my life. Next day she was much more quiet and, when the Doctor came to see her, he could find absolutely no sign of the growth; it had disappeared in the night, and a few days later she was 'discharged cured'!

"There she sat perched upon her pillow;"

G.P.I.—General Paralysis of the Inebriate

At one time, while I was still 'scrubbing', there were three patients in the East Wing who all had to have nasal feeds. One was a medical man with *G.P.I; one a tongue case and the third a baby with cerebrospinal meningitis. Unfortunately, all three feeds fell due at the same time so, as I had been asked to see to them all, as no Nurse is allowed to give one in Hospital unless she is known to be a real adept, without a Sister to superintend, I went round and told No. 1 that I would come a few minutes early; 2 I would go to at the right time and 3 a few minutes late. As it happened, I had never in my life given a nasal feed, and had only once seen it done, but, nevertheless, as I wore a blue frock and a cap with tails, I was bound to know all about it. But, in spite of the cap and frock, I had chosen to go first to the ward where there was a Staff Nurse who, I knew, had given them before and so would not need to be taught. I watched carefully and all went off as it should.

The great danger is, with an unconscious patient, that in passing the catheter one may, by accident, introduce it into the air passage and then the egg and milk and so forth, instead of going into the stomach, will find its way into the lungs, which would very speedily cause death by drowning if it were not noticed immediately and steps taken to rectify the mistake, and anyhow it would probably start a very severe attack of pneumonia whatever one did.

Next I chose the ward where the tongue case was, because the patient was conscious, as—though it is often more difficult to do with patients who can feel—they do at least cough the minute the catheter shows any signs of going in the wrong direction. The trouble with them is that sometimes they will cough just at the wrong moment and then they shoot the end that was intended to go down into their stomachs out of their mouths. I saw that done wonderfully neatly once by a suicide. He had taken to refusing his food and so was ordered nasal feeding. This went on quite peacefully for a time, as he knew it was no use to be violent, as he would merely have had a policeman to hold him down, but one day he discovered that, if he gave the least little cough at a certain moment, the end of the catheter came up into his mouth, instead of going on its way downwards. This he did, keeping his mouth shut and pretending that all had gone on as usual, till Nurse had started to pour the feed down, and then, when his mouth was quite full, he opened it and the result may be imagined! There was a regular deluge as the disgustingly eggy milk kept coming, even after his mouth was empty, as it was impossible to stop everything at once and withdraw the catheter without hurting him.

But the tongue case played no tricks of this sort. I went to the ward and found that, not only had Nurse never given a nasal feed, but she had got nothing ready and could not for the life of her think what would be wanted. She had been taught, like the rest of us at the 'Training Home', but had entirely forgotten. She was one of the intellectual kind of nurses who have been to College and can never remember or see the use of the practical side of anything. She could have drawn diagrams of any of her patients' internal arrangements and discribed [sic] minutely all the processes of digestion undergone by the feed when it once arrived in the stomach, but goodness only knows how she would have got it there if she had been left to herself; most probably she would have forgotten even to give it. Well, I told her what things she would need to give this feed with, and where to find them, as she seemed very vague on that subject too. I also told her that I was going away for about ten minutes and would expect to find everything ready when I came back.

I went to see my third feed, in 'baby land'. Here everything was ready but Nurse was so horribly nervous that, though she had given them before, she begged me to do it, at any rate the first time. Her former attempts had all been on conscious adults and this was an unconscious baby. So, seeing how frightened she was, I felt pretty well certain that she would make a mess of it and decided that, if anyone was going to kill the child, it had better be me. I knew I could keep my hand steady at any rate and that was something. I own I was nervous, but I made a dash for it, it was the only thing to be done to carry it through; if one hesitates one is sure to fail. When Nurse thanked me at the end, I did not tell her that it was my first performance; I thought it wiser to keep that to myself.

After that, I returned to the tongue case—it was more than ten minutes since I had left, but Nurse was still hovering round the cupboard in a doubtful sort of way. 'I think I have everything that you said you would want', she said, puckering up her brows and lolling against the doorpost. I went to the tray and found one or two things missing, which I asked

59

for, and then began to fit the catheter and funnel together, and was just about to start 'passing' it, when it struck me to ask 'I suppose you have the feed ready have you and not too hot?'. There was a silence and I looked up at her face, absolutely blank with amazement. 'The . . . the feed!', she stuttered. 'Yes, what did you think I was going to do with all this if I was not going to give him a feed?'. 'Oh, I forgot you would want anything to give him. What shall I get?'. 'Didn't you have any orders? Isn't it on the night sheet? Well, then look on his blue board, what does that say?'. 'Milk 2 pints, Eggs 3, Soup 1 pint. Shall I mix them all together and bring them?'. 'No! bring ℥ VIII [8 fluid ounces] of milk and one egg and a little salt, mix them together and warm them and mind the temperature is not to be any more than 99°F. What is written on the board is the amount to be given in 24 hours. How would you like to be made to swallow 3 eggs and 3 pints of fluid at one sitting?'. She did not think fit to answer to this, but simply allowed a look of wondering pity to wander over her face, as much as to say 'I wonder what is the matter with her, poor thing, she does seem cranky tonight, perhaps night duty does not agree with her'. When at last she was ready, I explained carefully what I was going to do and why and how.

When it was all over, I told her that I would arrive exactly at 4 a.m. to give the next feed and I would not expect to be kept waiting again. I returned as the clock struck 4 and she had managed to get out about half the necessary things, but nothing would hurry her and she kept on stopping to make the most irrelevant remarks and ask the most unheard-of questions on the value and uses of drugs and I can't remember what else. But I know I longed for a barge pole at the time to hurry her up with, but I did my best to answer her questions, as I always like to encourage an enquiring mind!

At 8, when I came for the third and last feed for that night, the only thing that was wrong was that Nurse had boiled the milk, so that the egg had curdled and the whole thing was much too hot, which caused some delay, but still it was better, and I told her that next night she must try to give the feeds herself, while I looked on. When the time came, I really did feel sorry for the poor patient, but nurse had to learn to do it sometime, and I thought the sooner the better, as she might not get another chance. To begin with, she persisted in standing in her own light and on the wrong side of the man. I asked if she was left-handed, but it was not that. Then she seemed to have great difficulty in holding the things. I can't think why, because her hands were quite big enough and invariably gave a jerk at the critical moment and so pulled the catheter out again, or else she stopped in the middle and so tickled the back of the poor man's throat, so that he was bound to cough the thing into his mouth. When this had happened five times I lost patience and took the things and did it myself. I felt quite an old hand by this time, but I was afraid Nurse might do some damage if I let her go on any longer. The same thing happened each time that night and the following day the patient was allowed to take his food by mouth and so I don't know if Nurse ever learnt to give nasal feeds or if she would still only tickle the back of her patients' throats.

Miss Martin as she came to see Matron —

Another very curious specimen of nurse was one I came across, just about this time too, but she is no longer at large—we returned her at the end of three months to the convent from which she came and where she had been brought up. Her name was Martin and she was Irish; also I noticed a look of despair on the face of the Staff Nurse in whose ward she was working. It was a very busy Men's Surgical and Martin was the only Probationer in that division. I had noticed her some weeks before in Matron's office, when she came for her first interview, and thought then that she was an unusual type. She was a quiet, gentle looking creature with her hair parted in the middle and drawn down smoothly over her ears. She had worn an old-fashioned dress of some black material with mauve flowers on it, a very full skirt and long waist and her hat was more like an early Victorian bonnet than anything else I had seen.

Miss Martin a few weeks later.

Now what a change was here—her hair was still parted, but on her head or rather sliding off it at the back was a very crooked cap, her print frock had strange fullnesses, where there should have been none, and the puffs of her sleeves, instead of being gathered in at the elbows, reached to her wrists. When she removed her white sleeves, which appeared only as cuffs below the enormous puffs above, there protruded what looked suspiciously like pink flannelette nightgown sleeves, and the tail of her dress and the corners of her apron dropped in a dejected manner as I stood and watched her sweep three times in a circle round her, just in front of the fire. I could not stop to investigate the subject any further, but I was profoundly sorry for the Staff Nurse whose only Probationer she was.

A night or two later, the Assistant Matron came to the room while we were having our meal and turned to me at once saying 'Sister, would you mind going along to Nurse Martin's room at about 10.30 to see if she has gone to bed? Last night I discovered her in the Nurses' Sitting Room when I went in to turn off the light there. She could not give me any reason why she had not gone to bed, except that she forgot, so if you would just go to her room every night to see that she has not forgotten again, it would be a great relief to me. I do not like the idea that people may be roaming about the Hospital in that way, when they are supposed to be in bed. There have been several minor thefts lately, too, and, though I don't for a moment think Nurse Martin is capable of stealing, she would naturally be suspected if she was found about after it was time for the lights to be out'. I said I would certainly do it, little thinking what a job I was letting myself in for at the time.

At 10.30 I went to Nurse's room; the light was still on, so I knocked and, getting no answer, I opened the door and there was Martin, standing fully dressed in the middle of the room, staring out of the window. I told her it was time her light was out and she must make haste into bed. She offered to put the light out at once, without waiting to undress, but I thought she had better do that first. Night after night I found her either wandering aimlessly about the passage, or doing things that were absolutely unnecessary in her room, but she was never in bed. Sometimes I had to pay her as many as three visits before I was sure she was safely in bed. One night I arrived to find her in her petticoats with every other conceivable garment strewn about the room and all the drawers open. I asked my usual question 'Why are you not in bed yet, Nurse, don't you know it is after half past ten?'. 'Oh, I am quite ready, Sister; shall I put out the light?'. 'But you are not undressed yet, Nurse; you don't mean to get into bed like that, do you?'. 'Oh, no, but I can't find my nightgown anywhere' and she fell on her knees in front of her chest of drawers and began raking over the contents as she spoke. 'I don't know what can have become of it; I think I must have sent it to the wash'. 'Well, Nurse, if that is the case, and you only have the one, I think you had better go to bed in something else tonight and get yourself another tomorrow, but make haste into bed now—I will be back in a few minutes to see if your light is out'.

Another night I found her standing staring blankly in front of her in a half-dressed condition and spread over her dressing table was a large white three-quarter-length serge coat, dripping wet. But whether she had been trying to wash it or had only got into her bath in it by mistake, I don't know or perhaps, like the French nuns, she had been taught at her convent that it was improper to take her bath without some covering and, failing a chemise, she had selected her great coat for the purpose.

One day the Staff Nurse of the ward she worked in told me that, when she went up to the theatre with an operation case, it was impossible to leave any instructions with Martin as to what the other patients might have for tea, or when to give the feeds and, as some afternoons she spent the greater part of her time in the theatre, it might have been serious, only just at that time there was a man up and able to help who was a steward on board one of the passenger ships that run from London to Scotland and he used to take and carry out any order Nurse gave. I don't know what Nurse would have done without him just then, as he was far more use than the Probationer and could always be trusted to do as he was asked, and often I used to see him making beds, sweeping, polishing or dusting, when I went through the ward. He was about 6 ft. 3 ins. in his stockings and was always known as 'Curley' on account of his hair. For a full month Nurse Martin stayed in that ward, but she seemed no better at the end of the time than she did at the beginning and, at the end of three months, she was told she might go as we could never make a nurse of her, however long we kept her.

One morning the Household Assistant came to see in great distress; she said that the 'Surgical Registrar' had come to her to ask who it was that looked after the night scrubbers. She was very much afraid that they must have been doing something that annoyed him in the offices, he seemed so cross. I had met the enraged gentleman once before and was not half so alarmed as the poor Household Assistant seemed to expect. Last time we had met he had complained that the scrubbers must have stolen some pens and blotting paper and that there were some crumbs on the desk and he did not like people eating in the office. I removed the crumbs for him and informed him that once I had seen one of my scrubbers trying to write out a list of the others' names and that, if he had seen the contortions she went through in the process and the final result of her effort, I did not think he would be likely to accuse her, or any of the others, who were not such good 'scollards' as she was, of being so in love with pens and blotting paper that they would wish to steal them, but that in the future it might be as well to remove all chance of temptation, by making his clerks put away their things before they went home, instead of leaving them all about the desks.

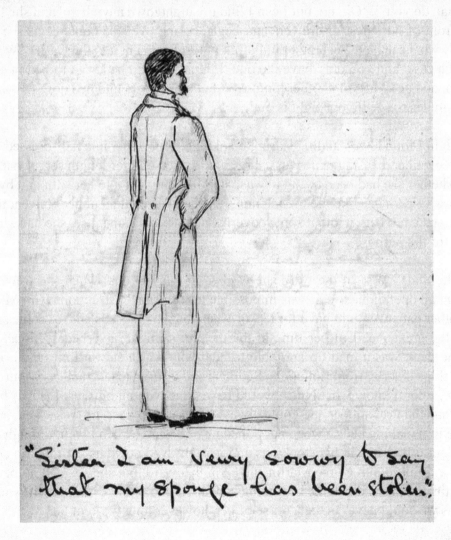

"Sister I am vewy sowwy to say that my sponge has been stolen".

This time, however, he looked much more serious. 'Sister, I am vewy sowwy to say that my sponge has been stolen. It was a large, abdominal sponge and I paid half a crown for it only yesterday. I left it in the basin last night and it has gone'. I told him that I, too, was sorry, but that I had not seen it myself, but would enquire of the scrubber who worked in his offices that night, in case she knew anything of the sponge. I did not think she would have taken it, as it did not seem to me that abdominal sponges would appeal to her much.

Next night I did enquire, but nobody seemed to have seen or heard of a sponge in those or any other of the offices. I hunted everywhere I could think of and came to the conclusion that it was quite as likely that the clerks had taken it to clean their pens or their boots on, as that the scrubbers had taken it to clean their faces, so at last I gave up the hunt.

" a 'olding me nose all the time - "

About a week later Mrs. Aitkin came to me with a beaming and triumphant smile 'Oh, Sister, you'll please excuse me, but I just remembered what may 'ave 'appened to that sponge'. 'Why, did you see it after all then, Mrs. Aitkin?'. 'Well, Sister, I thinks maybe I did and took it for some'ing nasty. I must say it was not much like a sponge, but Mrs. Schaffe 'ere she says it may 'ave been one, but he do keep such nasty things about this office sometimes—bones and insides and all sorts—and I sees some'ing and calls Mrs. Schaffe to come and look at this 'ere and says she "What be it Mrs. Aitkin?", and I says "Hit's just another of 'is nasty messes". It was down there, jus' by the slop pail, an' I thinks that he made a bad shot an' was just trying to throw hit in, so I takes two sticks, and shovels hit hup in the dus'pan. I would not touch hit with me fingers, hit looks too nasty and Mrs. Schaffe she says "Ugh, the nasty mess, you'd best put hit down the sink quick as you can afore Sister comes along and sees it", she says, 'So I puts it down, a 'olding me nose all the time, for fear it 'ad begun to smell, and now it warn't nothin' arter all, but the poor gentleman's sponge, but I niver seed the like before—it warn't natural, But, as I says to Mrs. Schaffe, just as you come along, 'e shouldn't a lef' hit hon the floor down there with the slop pail ef 'e'd wanted te keped it'. So I warned the old lady that, in future, if she found anything curious about, she had better keep it for my inspection, before deciding that it was nasty and must be thrown away, and I also informed the Registrar of the fate of his precious sponge and suggested that he might find a better place to keep the next one.

Not long after this, I went back on day duty again and found I was to go to the same 'Men's Medical' I had been in where Mrs. Love ruled the scullery, and the Probationers when she got the chance. It was only about a week from the time when Sister's holiday was to be, which meant that I would most likely be left in charge during that time. I rather dreaded the ordeal, especially as the two Staff Nurses were still both there and on no better terms than when I was in the ward on the former occasion.

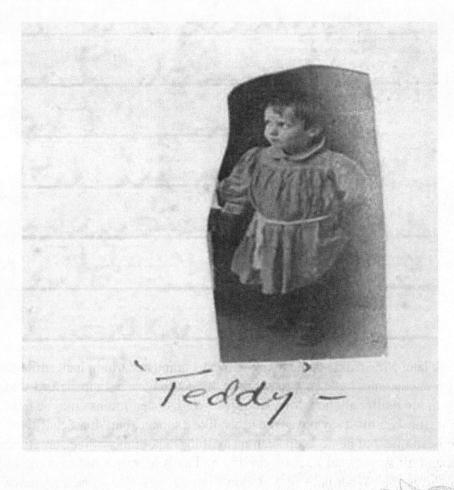

'Teddy'—

The first morning, I was sitting on the coal box, conversing with a small boy who was just allowed up, when I felt a gentle pull at the tail of my cap and a little voice exclaim, in a tone that was half shy and half triumphant, 'I 'members you'. I turned and there was Teddy, but such a different Teddy from the one I remembered a few months back. He was up and dressed and looking remarkably well and by this time was quite a well-known character all over Hospital. He was rarely to be found when wanted in his own ward as, if he could not persuade the doctors to take him on their rounds in the other ward or down to their own rooms, he went with the porters. The coalman was his special friend, as he used to give him rides on the coal trucks among the buckets and, when we did get him back, he really was a sight for the Gods! Another of Teddy's failings was greediness, not over his meals, but everything else. He was a regular scavenger and went round the whole floor, eating up fruit, biscuits, sweets or anything else he could manage to extract from the other patients or their visitors and, as the nurses in the further ward always gave him bread and jam or cake when they had their own tea, and the doctor invariably brought him chocolate, it was not wonderful [sic] that we had great trouble at times in making him eat his own meals. Breakfast was not so bad as the others, as he had been in bed all night and had had no chance of scavenging before 6.30 a.m., but for all his wickedness Teddy was a darling and never bore one any grudge if one put him to bed for being naughty, or took away his sweets if he seemed to be overeating himself worse than usual. He would merely go and take somebody else's sweets, instead! Or invent something still more naughty to do, as soon as he was up again but, if he really knew that he had been naughty and deserved to go to bed, he retired under the bedclothes and cried, till he either went to sleep or could tell the person who had put him there that he was sorry. One night, I had put him to bed in disgrace and he went to sleep before he could make up his mind to 'be sorry' and I went off duty. In the morning, when he woke, Night Nurse could not think what was the matter with him, as he refused to talk, or get up, or eat his breakfast. She thought at first he was feeling ill, but there seemed nothing wrong with him, then she thought he was sulking and tried to tease him, but nothing moved him until 8.30 a.m., when I came on duty. As soon as prayers were over he called, so I went to see what he wanted. When I got close to him, he sidled up to the edge of the bed and put his arms round my neck and pulled my head down to him and with a beaming smile, said 'I's sorry, Sister. Now you can dress me in my new boots and I can have an egg for tea'. In about ten minutes from that time, he was racing up and down the ward in his new boots, cheeking all the men, with a bannana [sic] in one hand and about three or four biscuits in the other, bent on making up for lost time, both in eating and noise.

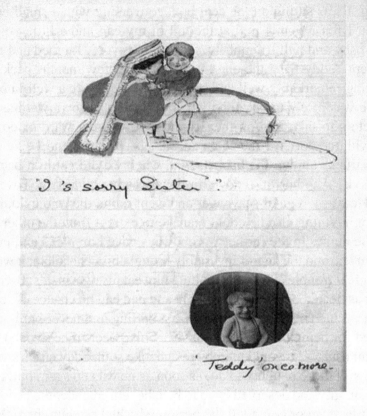

'I 's sorry Sister'?

'Teddy' once more.

Nothing went seriously wrong while Sister was away for her holiday, except that some of the ward money was found to be missing when she came back. She and I went through the accounts before she left and I made the necessary additions and went through everything again just before she came back. Then, two days later, Sister came to me to ask if I was sure it was £5-odd that I had left in her drawer, because she could only find £4-odd. I was practically certain that I was right in saying £5, so we hunted everywhere, but there was no sign of that missing pound and at last we agreed that we would have to make it up out of our own pockets, as we could not let the ward or patients suffer. One of us must have been careless, as it seemed an impossibility for the money to have been stolen, as the drawer was always kept locked and visitors, patients or ward maids must have been noticed at once if they had gone to Sister's desk, besides the Staff Nurses and 'Pro Staffs' were the only people who knew where the key was kept. The mystery was solved about a year later, but that is quite another story and so must wait.

When I left this ward I was sent down to the Receiving Room, to take the Assistant R.R. Sister's place while she was away for her holiday. Here the work is utterly different from anywhere else. I had a few duties in Matron's Office, such as stamping envelopes, folding papers, cleaning slates and answering the telephone while I was there, which was not often. At other times I was either in the Receiving Room, taking the regular Sister's place when she went for meals, or off duty, or else in the Out-Patients Department: two mornings a week, in the aural theatre, which brought back my Probationer days very forcibly, specially when I saw our Surgeon stowing the towels in his pockets again, as of old, and shouting for 'Sister' to get him all sorts of instruments by names of his own invention.

One of my most amusing recollections of those days was a day when I was in the 'Recovery Room', where the children came to recover from the anæsthetic before being returned to their parents. There were several cases to be kept in hospital for the night. One was a nasal case and had to be taken over to the ward fairly early in the morning; the others did not go till a good deal later. The first one, and the last, happened to go to the same ward, the one I worked in when not in Out-Patients. When I arrived with the second patient, I could see no nurse anywhere, so I put the child in the bed prepared for her and sent a convalescent patient to sit beside her until somebody came, then I looked through to the other division, where the first patient I had taken over was, and there was a very new Probationer standing beside her, looking terribly frightened. The minute she saw me, she called out 'Oh, Nurse, please do come, I don't know what is happening here!'. So I went. The probationer exclaimed again 'Oh, I don't know what it is, but something seems to be coming up from inside, out of her mouth'.

"I don't know what is happen-ing here!"

This sounded rather alarming but, in reality, it was nothing but a very discoloured strip of gauze plugging that had been in the woman's nose. The greater part was still there, but the patient had been snuffling and coughing so violently that the innermost end had been forced down her throat and then coughed out at her mouth and both she and the unfortunate

Probationer thought that it was a portion of her own internal anatomy run loose! I sent the Probationer to fetch scissors and forceps and one or two things I needed to put matters straight, but she never returned! So, again, I had recourse to another convalescent patient who fetched what I needed, and then sat beside the woman till somebody more capable appeared, as I had to return to Out-Patients.

But now I was no longer a Probationer, and stayed in the theatre all the time, to look after the Surgeons instead of the patients, which was quite an easy job, as I had so often watched the Sister when I was a Probationer, and had learned to keep the largest coat for the smallest man and knew nicknames, as well as real ones, for all the instruments in use up there.

Two other duties I had; one was 'Obstetric O.P.s' for Dr. Andrews and the other Classes! I had to teach the rising generation of Probationers what lecturers had been trying to make them understand, which was sometimes a very difficult task. From 8 till 9 p.m. on various nights of the week, some 12 or 14 Probationers used to come to my room in various conditions of drowsiness, some because they were on night duty and had only just tumbled out of bed, others because they were on day and were longing to tumble in, and it was truly wonderful what strange conditions of muddle most of their brains were in. One had to explain the simplest words to some, others had made neither head nor tail of the notes they had taken at the lecture the week before and seemed incapable of even taking any down from dictation, and most needed teaching as if they were children of 5, instead of grown women, but woe betide the unfortunate teacher if she let them see she thought them stupid or even, with some, tried to make them give a sensible answer to an easy question if the first shot had been wrong!

They were offended or would not be bullied!—or suddenly become too nervous to answer anything and melted into tears. There were, of course, a few brilliant exceptions, who behaved like ordinary human beings and could even put up with being laughed at if they made very absurd blunders. Then there were the really clever ones and it was a dreadful temptation to race on to interesting subjects with them and leave the others to flounder, but of course this could never be done, as one had to take them as one found them and *make* them pass their exams, but I felt the whole time that I ought to be apologising to those who could understand what I said for talking such nonsense. I had one most depressing young woman who, whenever I stated a fact or made any attempt to rub something special in particularly carefully, always started asking questions about something quite different and never knew what I had been saying. She had had previous training and thought it beneath her to stick to the subject in hand.

But what I really did enjoy was being in the Receiving Room itself. There one felt as if one was in the centre of the universe and had a hand in the making of history and lives. Every patient that ever comes to the Hospital has first to go to the Receiving Room and there his or her fate is settled, whether it be a little good advice only or advice and a dose, or a card, or a

letter for Out-Patients, where they will be expected to attend regularly, or in the more serious cases an admission ticket for the wards.

It is in the Receiving Room that they are seen first by a 'Receiving Room Officer', who diagnoses their case, and it is at the Receiving Room desks that they get prescriptions or tickets and their place in the Hospital allotted. If one is interested in any special case, one can generally follow it up from the Receiving Room, as one knows who was 'taking in' and, therefore under which Doctor the case was admitted and to which ward, and it is here in the Receiving Room that the Doctors congregate when waiting for their 'Chiefs', or other things equally important, such as meeting one another to make up numbers for Bridge etc.

Some of our people attend almost as regularly as if they were real 'Out-Patients'—they come once a week for a dose or after a drinking bout. One old lady was always turning up in a very merry condition and used to entertain the other women in the waiting room by dancing and singing for them!

"Dancing + Singing for them".

Then there was a man and his wife who generally came alternately with broken heads and cut faces. The last time I saw them, they arrived within a few minutes of each other, both brought by the Police, she with her forehead cut open from a kick—he with both ankles damaged and a knock on the head because, having kicked her and had a bang with the poker in return, he had jumped out of the window, because he thought she was dead! We stitched her up and let her go. He, catching sight of her alive after all, felt better and bolted, damaged ankles and all, with the Police in pursuit. I am afraid our porters did not help as they should have done in the capture as our friend managed to get out of the Hospital gates and some way down Whitechapel Road before the Police managed to tackle him and reduce him to order. The 'lady' who came with a nasty bite on her cheek and, when asked if a dog did it, answered 'No, another loidy', was not a regular attendant—nor was the one who, on seeing my chameleon, exclaimed 'Oh, I've got 'eeps of them things at 'ome, they runs roun' and roun' the ceiling'—but they were quite amusing when they did come.

I was a month in the R.R. as Assistant and then, after an interval which I spent in a Men's Surgical ward, returned to take the Head Receiving Room Sister's place. The ward I went to was in the basement and opened into a yard, politely known as the 'Park', because Sister had planted green tubs and boxes with shrubs and flowers, so that the patients would have something nice to look at when their beds were taken out. Sister was a well-known character throughout the Hospital and to see and hear her instructing a Probationer in her duties, or even a Houseman or a visiting Surgeon, was a treat.

I was in the ward one day when Sister was showing a new Probationer how to get a patient ready to be taken up to the theatre. Sister, the patient and the Probationer were all at one end of the ward and the cupboards, where the necessary things were kept, were at the other when they started. 'Now, Nurse, go to the left-hand cupboard and on the second shelf you will see some theatre coats; fetch one long red coat'. She fetched it. 'Now, will you go to the same cupboard and on the same shelf you will see some blankets—will you please fetch one large theatre blanket'. She did so. 'Now if you look again on that shelf you will see some small blankets—bring one'. She brought it. 'If you look a little further along behind the small blankets you will see some red blankets—we must have one of those'. Behind something else were the head wraps, one of which had to be brought. On another shelf were shoes—she was allowed to bring the two shoes together but nothing more. Then a pair of stockings. Then one long mackintosh, then one short one, then another, not two together, then three theatre tins, one at a time, finally the patient's chart boards. To get all these things collected, one at a time, from the further end of the ward, took a considerable length of time, but time was no object to Sister, even when the porters were waiting with the trolley to take the patient upstairs to the theatre! Her object was to make the Probationer fetch the rights things and remember what they were and that certainly was accomplished.

I learned a great many things from poor old Sister, though not in the painful way of the Probationers but by watching Sister and then, if she did anything unusual, asking why, for— although some of her methods were a little antiquated—she was a thoroughly good Nurse and had very good reasons for the odd things she did and never minded explaining anything one liked to ask her about, from the method of giving an enema to how to treat the most serious operation case, or even how the operation should be done.

There are many funny stories told of what happened at different times in that ward, but none so funny as those told by Sister herself. Sometimes, after the work was finished in the evening, and if Sister was not too tired, she might be persuaded to recount some of her experiences, one of which always entertained me enormously. A long time ago, when she was first made Sister of her ward, she had five Probationers. At the time she told me the story, two were elderly Private Staff Nurses and three were Sisters, but as long ago as it had happened, none of them could bear so much as to hear 'iced coffee' mentioned. It was one afternoon, when Sister's favourite Surgeon was operating. As usual she had made him some coffee and put it in the icebox, as he liked it iced on a hot day, and there were cakes in Sister's room but, unfortunately, he had to leave hospital in such a hurry that he had no time for coffee or cakes and so Sister, not liking them to be wasted, had told her five nurses that, if they hurried up with their work that evening, they might sit down and finish them up, just before she came back on duty at 8 o'clock. When she arrived, what was her surprise to find all the lights full on and the patients sitting up in bed, trying to peer into the other division, but no nurses! She hurried through and there they all were, sitting round the table in various attitudes of misery and collapse. She called to them to know what was the matter, but only groans answered her. She went and shook the nearest, who moaned 'iced coffee' and the rest groaned in chorus.

Iced coffee!

Sister looked round the table; there were cups with the remains of a brownish fluid in the bottoms and a jug with the same and the remains of cakes, but how could iced coffee have had this effect on five ordinarily healthy women? Suddenly an idea occurred to her; she picked up the jug and sniffed and then flew to the icebox and looked in—there was the coffee still untouched! She fled to the oven and looked in—it was empty! When she had gone off duty she had left a jug there with an infusion of poppy heads in it, that she had been making for one of the men, because he had toothache.

The next thing was that she sent for the Houseman and the Assistant Matron; the nurses were given emetics and walked up and down the yard, in turns, to keep them awake. But how they got teased when they had recovered! It never transpired how five reasonable women took tepid poppy heads and water for iced coffee, or why they drank two cups each, for it is a filthy concoction. It is even rather difficult to understand why they looked in the oven for an iced drink of any sort but, if ever you want to prove the truth of the story, you have only to ask any one of the five whether they liked iced coffee or not and you will soon find out. But it takes Sister to tell the story properly.

Another rather amusing thing happened, but that was quite recently. It was one day when there was a new Ward Maid. She had been on trial there for a few days and had been told very severely the afternoon before that if a visiting Surgeon appeared in the ward she must disappear *at once*, whatever she might be doing. So this afternoon she was quite prepared.

She was scrubbing the ward and, as she emerged from between two beds on her hands and knees, she suddenly saw the Surgeon but, unluckily, there was no means of escape, for he had come in quietly and was now between her and the scullery. There was only one thing to be done—she could not face Sister's wrath and be seen, so she hurriedly collected the pail and brush, and all the other utensils she had, and slipped with them under the nearest bed. The students and nurses saw her and there was a suppressed whisper and giggle. Sister and the Surgeon could not think what was the matter—nobody seemed to be attending to them—but the procession proceeded round the ward and came to the very bed where the poor Ward Maid was hidden. Suddenly, he, too, noticed a bit of skirt and a foot protruding from under the bed, but he just managed to keep his countenance and beat a dignified retreat. Then out crawled the poor woman, just under Sister's nose, as she was scolding one of the nurses for not behaving better and there was a most tremendous explosion.

Another day, it happened that two men were taken in who had both been playing football and had both damaged their right legs in exactly the same way and, when the Surgeon went round after looking at them both, and saying what he thought would be the best treatment for them, he turned to Sister, smilingly, asking for approval but to his surprise she did not give it, but said she thought some other method preferable and, as Sister was a very privileged person, the Surgeon suggested that they should each have a leg and treat it as they thought best. Next week, when the Surgeon came round again, Sister greeted him with a beaming smile and, hurrying him towards the beds, said 'Now, Mr . . . . if you will come over here, we can compare our legs'—at which all the students burst into a roar of laughter.

On their way to compare legs!

When I left this ward, I went back to the R.R. for a time and then to another Men's Surgical ward, where I took the holiday duty. As a rule, the Sister of this ward had her holiday arranged for the same time as the Senior Surgeon, as he always hated having strange Sisters in the theatre and trusted almost entirely to Sister's memory, rather than his own, when seeing patients in the wards, but it happened this year that it could not be arranged and so he had to put up with me. Sister did her very best to instruct me before she went and the Staff Nurse was most kind and helpful whenever she could be, but neither of them could possibly make me remember things that had happened and patients that had been operated upon before I even came to the Hospital. So now and then we got into difficulties but, on the whole, things went fairly smoothly, after I had proved myself capable of shaking out the carbolic gauze correctly and handing the right number of pieces of wool to him in the theatre without having to be told.

The first day up in the theatre was a revelation to me. When we arrived (our case was an abdominal and would be a fairly big operation) there was another of the same sort still in the theatre, just being stitched up, but the minute we arrived, the Surgeon handed the job on to his Houseman and came to have a look at us and also sent a Dresser out to fetch in two little Out-Patients, who had come up for some form of tenotomy, which they had done sitting on the slabs at the side of the theatre. I bandaged one and a Dresser the other and then, to my surprise and bewilderment, I found the Surgeon had started operating on my case and the other Sister and Nurse were busy making off with all the clean bowls and receivers, which I had to recapture in a hurry as they seemed bent on only leaving me their old, dirty ones! We had three or four cases done that day and there always seemed to be at least two in the theatre at once, two in the anæsthetising room and another two waiting in the passage. It was just like a nightmare, but one gets used to it in time and even enjoys the rampage if one goes on long enough.

The week before Christmas again found me in the Women's Surgical ward where I had been twice before, working as hard and as fast as ever, but suddenly one of the Office Sisters was taken ill and another Assistant Sister, who happened to know her work, was moved from the ward she was in to take her place. Then the Sister of that ward started influenza and I was moved down there, already feeling rather dilapidated. I no sooner arrived than the Staff Nurse went off duty with a bilious attack and I had to send the 'Pro Staff' off with a bad finger and a Probationer tried climbing on the sink in the scullery and fell off and hit her head so hard that she got concussion, so I was left with nearly nobody on Christmas Eve, feeling very seedy myself and with all the decorations to do, Father Christmas's bag to make up and all the teas to arrange for that day and the next. Some students came to help with the decorations and I retired to the top of the stepladder in the lobby to put on the lamp shades and to be as far out of the way as possible, for I hated the very sight of everybody.

Christmas Day came—we were taking in—and both Sister and the Staff Nurse just managed to struggle out from the Sick Room, which only increased our work, as we had to run their errands as well as our own. I remember practically nothing of what went on in the shape of entertainments etc. All I knew was that we took in two or three new cases and I was thankful when I had to go up to the theatre with one of them, as I was at least out of the crowd and the noise. When the entertainments were over, and we were putting the patients and beds back in their places, I found that it was impossible to get round the ends of the beds without holding on to them and I knew I was dead tired, but there was an anæsthetic to be done in the ward very shortly, so I did not dare to go away and sit down for fear of not being able to persuade myself to get up again when the time came, so I just went on doing things till the nurses went off and the Houseman came. At last I went off duty and crept into bed. I knew I had a temperature, but could not be bothered to take it.

Next morning I felt sure it had gone down ever so much and went on duty as usual but, when I appeared, the Sister from the next ward bundled me into her room and produced a thermometer and then went to the office, returning shortly with orders for me to go to the Sick Room at once, as Matron did not like her Sisters go be on duty with temperatures of 102. I often wondered what it had been the day before when I really thought it was high. I spent five days in bed in the Sick Room and then had a week week's sick leave and came back feeling miserable, but that mostly wore off after a time, and only returned badly when I was told that Matron wished me to be in the Office for a time.

I will not say much about that, beyond that I hated the office and at the end of about three months I went and had an interview with Matron, with the result that she said that, if I really thought I would rather, I might go to 'Marie Celeste' and then return on the Private Staff, but that I must understand that, once I had settled to do so, I could never change my mind and I can assure you *that* did not make me hesitate even for a moment. Most people seemed to think I was mad at the time, but they were all bound to confess that I took ten years of my age off with the tails of my cap.

In 'Marie Celeste' I started late in May on the district. The Sisters fought like cats and dogs, and the nurses were not much better, but I loved every bit of it, even the dirt and sleepless nights and the fleas. I felt as if I had just been let loose out of a cage. I even went the length of trying to teach the other nurses to turn somersaults over a bar in the passage by our bedrooms, in the hopes that it might improve their tempers, and it did—they got ever so much better after a short time.

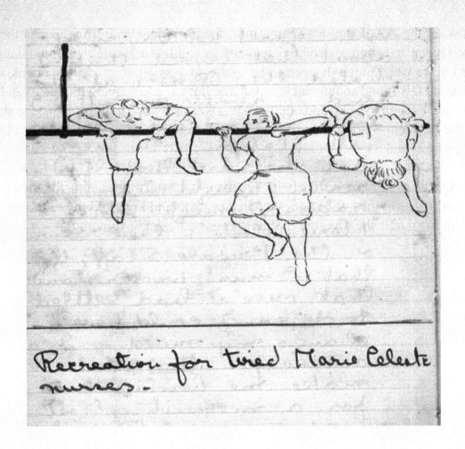

Recreation for tired Marie Celeste nurses.

Just at first I felt I was looked upon with a certain amount of suspicion by the other nurses, but it soon wore off, and one of them told me it was only that they were afraid I might be like Miss . . . . , another 'blue' who was up there whom they did not like, as she had enquired who was to scrub her mackintosh and apron and do her bag the first time she came in from a case. Also she always looked sulky and saw the gloomy side of life and was always most careful not to do more than her share of any of the work that was going.

The first morning I was taken round my 'district' by the nurse who was just leaving it. She was very tired and very vague as to where the different people lived, so it took us some time to get round our nine babies and mothers, but we managed just to get back in time for second dinner and scrambled in, in our cloaks and bonnets. That afternoon there was a lecture and I had to be instructed in various things to do with bags and babies and did not go out again, neither did I go out that night, but it was almost the only one that I did spend entirely in bed.

But before I go any further, I must mention one thing that happened while I was in the Office, which, in my general disgust at being there, I had forgotten. That was a visit from Queen Alexandra and the Dowager Empress of Russia. There was great excitement for, not only were they to go round the Hospital, but were also to have lunch in the Committee Room with Matron, her two Assistants and the Chairman. The Office Sisters were to wait at table, in place of the men they generally took with them. It really was all very comical.

To begin with, the Royal carriages came in at the back door and drove across the garden, so that the Queen and Empress could disembark in comfort and safety, with no danger from bombs or knives which might happen to be in the possession of unfriendly aliens, of which we have a good few round about our Hospital. The lawn was covered with nurses and patients who were well enough to be up and out; the paths were crowded with students, the steps were lined by the Resident Staff and, at the top was Matron, backed by the Visiting Physicians, Surgeons, porters and a general crowd.

Just as the Queen and Empress were being received at the top of the stairs, the Sister who was standing next to me at the Office door clutched my arm and implored me to look at 'A most horrible looking man': she was sure that he was an anarchist or something.

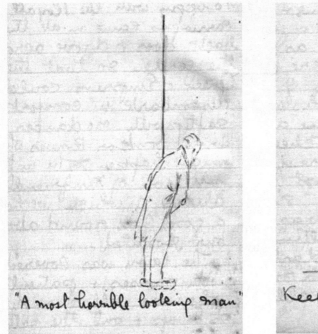

"A most horrible looking man"

Keeping his eye on the man.

Then she made a dart across the passage to one of our most staid and elderly porters and begged him to keep an eye on the man—which he did, and I don't think he would have let our horrible looking friend do much harm if he had wanted to, as he hung round and dogged his steps as anxiously as a fond mother might do the first tottering steps of her beloved infant.

The first ward they went to was the children's and it was almost impossible to get them out again and certainly the children were very charming. There was one little girl who had heard that the Queen was coming and was very anxious to give her a bunch of violets but, unfortunately, she had to go and be operated on that day and, when the Queen arrived, she was only just coming round from the anæsthetic, so the Chairman asked her to avoid that cot but, when the child saw everybody going away from where she was, she set up a most pitiful wail and would not be pacified until the Queen was brought back and she had presented her with a very squashed and dead little bunch of violets that the child had been clutching in her hand all the time she had been up in the theatre and under the anæsthetic. Of course the Queen had to wear them and the next child she went to, seeing she had two bunches, demanded some of her flowers and got some of the unsquashed bunch. Another small person, seeing the Queen's hand resting on the side of its cot, crawled up and kissed it and won great applause but, when he asked every other person in turn who came up if he might kiss theirs too, it turned into rather a joke.

After going through various other wards, the visitors were taken down to Out-Patients to see the Light Department, where the lamp the Queen had presented to us was. The crowd in the big waiting hall was enormous. Never before had so many of our Out-Patients thought fit to come on the same day, but how they had discovered beforehand that there was anything unusual going to happen that day was a puzzle, as nobody had been told. All sorts of conditions came and, when the moment arrived, small girls were hurried out in the middle of being examined and held up in a half-dressed condition by their doctors to see the Queen go through. One old Russian Jewess at the back of the crowd, when she heard that the Dowager Empress was there too, spat furiously and called out 'O, I would like to stick a knife into her', but that was the only unfriendly remark that was heard all the time they were going round.

Some of the Out Patient crowd.

After visiting the Light Department and various other parts of Out-Patients, lunch was served. We were sent for from the Office, there were five of us, and we waited in a row, just in front of a row of red-coated footmen, or some such people, who were going to act as prompters to us, in case we forgot, or did not know how, to hand the dishes. We were just by the door and, when the Royal party appeared, there was an enormous amount of shuffling, bobbing and ducking on our part, which was all intended to be courtsiying [sic]. It was a very merry lunch party and the Queen chattered and chaffed all the time and even dipped her fingers in some mineral water she had and flicked it across the table at one of the Assistant Matrons, as she said she was sure she was a Suffragette. We upset the poor red-coated footmen very much for totally disregarding all etiquette.

Shuffling bobbing + ducking –

The Queen seemed to enjoy herself enormously and took two helpings of nearly everything. The rest of the company, though they were not bound to eat the same quantities, should try, by rights, to spin out each course, till the Queen had finished her supply but, instead of that, one of the Sisters in excess of zeal hurriedly changed plates and presented fresh courses, until some of the unwary revellers found themselves devouring cheese, when they should still have been at the chicken stage! At the end of the meal, the Chairman produced the Hospital Visitor's Book for the Queen to sign, which she did, inscribing her name and age next birthday and announcing that she would be tomorrow! 60-something I think it was. When this was over, the footmen presented us with various garments of outdoor attire to put on the Queen and Empress and their ladies. I had the Queen's feather boa. When I put it on to fasten it properly, she had to take off the flowers she was wearing and put them down on the table and, instead of taking the same again, she took a fresh bunch from a vase and, after she had gone and we had all made our bobs again, I went back and picked the flowers off the table, when I suddenly found myself the centre of an excited crowd. 'Oh, give me half, give me one, give *me* some too'. 'If you give me some of the Queen's, I will give you all these ones the Empress was wearing'. So I gave a good many away and got some of the others in return. Then we went to our lunch and finally helped to cheer the whole party off and felt very pleased, as the great man in livery, who stands about near the Queen, said he had never before seen the Empress really look happy and at her ease, and she certainly did here.

* * * * *

QUEEN AND EMPRESS AT THE LONDON HOSPITAL *on 9th MARCH 1907*.

The Queen and the Empress Marie paid a private visit on Saturday to the London Hospital, of which the Queen is president. Attended by members of their suites, their Majesties drove down to the hospital from Buckingham Palace, arriving at midday. They were received by Lord Stanley (treasurer of the institution), the Hon. Sydney Holland (chairman) and by the secretary (Mr. E. W. Morris), Miss Luckes (the matron) and other officials. The Empress was anxious to see something of the conditions under which English hospital nurses live and carry on their work and a start was therefore made with the nurses' home, where some 50 nurses were assembled. Both Royal visitors made a point of speaking separately to every one of the nurses and asking a variety of questions as to their work. The hospital encourages its nurses to practice the art of cooking for sick inmates and at the time of the visit several of them were engaged in the preparation of "sick men's trays". There were about a dozen trays, all decorated with lilies of the valley and violets. The Royal visitors next crossed to the hospital buildings proper. These cover an area of eight acres, which is intersected at intervals by narrow streets, over which or under which are bridges or tunnels connecting the different parts of the hospital; but the Queen and the Empress preferred to walk across Oxford Street. In the quadrangle by which the main buildings are approached from the grounds, every available nurse and some hundreds of students were assembled to greet the Royal visitors, while every balcony was crowded with nurses, patients and attendants. Their Majesties inspected the site which has been set apart for a statue of the Queen; and her Majesty expressed pride and pleasure that the first public statue of herself in London should find place outside the great East End hospital and should be intended to commemorate the fact of her presidency of the institution.

After seeing some of the apartments in the main building, their Majesties expressed a wish to go to the children's ward, and were accordingly conducted to the accident department. Here their Majesties visited every cot, and spoke to all the children. Next they passed to the lying-in ward, where some of the poorest and most destitute of Whitechapel's poor are tended during confinement and convalescence. Here the visitors again spoke to every occupant of the ward and asked questions as to the names of the children, the dates of birth, the mothers' plans, the size of their families and their own progress.

Luncheon was served in the committee-room, where a table had been laid for 12 persons. The Queen sat between Lord Stanley and Mr. Sydney Holland, while the Empress Marie took her place at Lord Stanley's right. The luncheon was served by sisters, assisted by three of the Royal footmen. After luncheon, the Queen and the Empress were conducted to the outpatients department to see something of the Finsen light treatment for lupus, the first installation of the light having been presented to the hospital by the Queen. The Finsen light

SEE OVER →

department was reached through the surgical ward, where there were 56
occupied beds, all the occupants of which received a kindly word from
the Royal ladies.   While their Majesties were in the ward two operation
cases were brought in.   The patients were just recovering from
anaesthetics, but both were able to recognise and answer the questions
of their Majesties.   In the Finsen light department also the Royal
visitors spoke to all the patients and displayed the keenest interest.
Dr. Sequeira, the head of the department, exhibited photographs of
some of the worst cases and, in order to show in the most practical
manner, the efficacy of the treatment, he had summoned by telegraph
some of the patients cured, whom the Queen congratulated.

     After visiting the ophthalmic wards, their Majesties left
the hospital at 3.15 to return to the Palace, and were most
enthusiastically cheered by a crowd which had assembled in the streets.
Beford leaving the hospital they signed the visitors book.

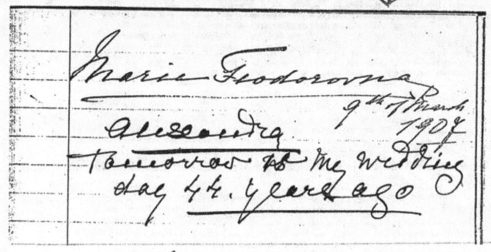

MARCH 9TH - 1907.

PHOTO COPY OF LONDON HOSPITAL VISITORS BOOK
(QUEEN ALEXANDRA & HER COMMENT, REGARDING HER, —
"WEDDING-DAY," 44 YEARS AGO)

Account of the visit as published in an unknown source and annotated by Tony Shephard.

* * * * *

Some little time back I started to describe my time up in the 'Lying-In Ward, 'Marie Celeste'. It is a difficult subject to write about to anybody who has not worked there, as almost all that is funny or interesting is so in a tecnical [*sic*] way and the only language that expresses it properly is either tecnical [*sic*] too or slang, and Hospital slang at that. For instance, the first case I went out to was a very interesting one from the Doctor's and Nurse's point of view and would be discribed [*sic*] as follows to one who 'knew'. She was a primip with a placenta previa [*sic*] and A.P.H. and we could not bring her in as there was too much dilatation to be safe to move her, so Sister sent for the J.R.A. and he put in a Champetier's bag. We were out about six hours—luckily the child was VI presentation and the placenta only partly over the '*os*' [bone, in French], so as soon as there was full dilatation and the bag came out, the J.R.A. got to work with his forceps—axis-traction—and the child was soon born. Luckily there was no R.P. beyond the inevitable tear and no P.P.H.

Of course, all that sounds double Dutch to most people and it looked and sounded nothing but a very messy kind of chaos to me at the time, seeing that it was my first case, but I was quite pleased, in spite of my utter bewilderment, as the J.R.A., otherwise the Junior Resident

Accoucher [*sic*], said he had very rarely met a nurse who 'did not turn a bit green at her first case, even when it was fairly ordinary, and this was anything but that, and I had not turned a hair', which was true, not even when he leant against me and nearly pushed me out of the window! I had been much too busy for that, trying to hold the lady still and at the same time avoid getting quite kicked over the end of the bed while the J.R.A. was busy attending to other matters.

By the time all was over it was dark and, as we were right down in Wapping, the J.R.A. offered us a lift home in his cab (he is always allowed a cab at Hospital expense as his bag is far too bulky to be carried by any man, be he ever so willing). When his cab came, it was a hansom, so first Sister was stowed away and then, as the J.R.A. was a large and heavy man, he was put in next and I was piled upon the top, with my head nearly sticking out of the trapdoor in the roof. The doors were then shut and the bag firmly fixed outside so that by no effort of our own could we possibly get out, unless by chance I might have mounted a little higher and squeezed out through the top! And so we drove home and were extracted by the Hospital porters when we arrived.

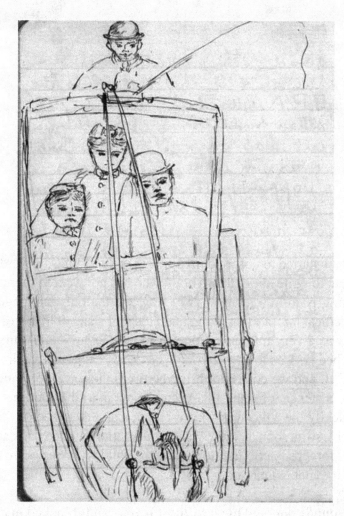

My next case was another 'abnormal' one, that is to say we had send for the J.R.A. again, but this time, only because there was more than the 'inevitable tear' and she had to have some stitches put in. She was also what we call a 'B.B.A.', which means that the baby was born before our arrival, for which mischance the mother got well scolded and told that, as we were not there when it first put in its appearance, we could be in no way responsible for it and would not even wash it. It had become necessary to make this a rule, because we found that the women put off sending for the nurses until they were sure of their arriving too late to insist on their washing or having an enema before the baby arrived, as those were the two things they hated most of anything that happened on those occasions. Unfortunately, this particular woman had thought fit to deposit herself and the baby on the floor, instead of the bed, and Sister and I had no end of trouble in getting them safely transferred to their proper place before the doctor came.

After this I had a run of fairly normal cases. For the first half dozen or so one is always taken out by a Sister, then if one appears to be fairly capable, one is sent out with one of the Senior Nurses, first simply to assist her by doing as one is told, later to be assisted by them and, finally, one is promoted to taking out one's own juniors and trying to instruct them in the ways they should go.

I suppose I had been up about a week when I had my first 'all night sitting', that is to say Sister and I started out late at night and still were in attendance next morning. Everything was perfectly all right, though slow so, at the end of about 7 hours, Sister thought she would like to go home and have some breakfast and off she went, leaving me with instructions to send for her at once if I wanted her or felt nervous at any time and, if she was not back, to let her know when things had got to a certain stage. If I had done as she said, and sent for her as soon as I felt nervous, she would never have left the house, as it was the first time I had ever been left entirely by myself to watch a case; but, as it happened, nothing occurred to really alarm me and I did not send for her until the moment arrived at which Sister had told me to send for her. Then I sent a note or 'flagged' as we called it. After that I became really frightened, as the baby began arriving so much faster than ever I had expected; in fact it positively raced into the world and turned up just at the same moment as Sister and, luckily, without any mishap.

It was nearly 12 by the time we got back to the Hospital so that, by the time I had had a bath and dressed and tidied my room and my bag, it was about dinner time, so I had no chance of starting out on my district to wash the babies. After dinner I asked if I could go, but found that all the other nurses had had cases between the time I went out the night before and when I had come back, so I was at the top of the list again and, as a card came in at that moment, I had to go off to another case. Luckily for me, it was a short one and I was back by about 4 for tea but, even then, I was not to be allowed to go off to my district as Dr. Andrews was coming to give a lecture about 5 and so I had to wait again and he was late, so that it was quite 7 p.m. before I started out.

I had nine babies to wash and a corresponding number of mothers to see to, but hoped that at any rate a few might have been attended to by their own friends and relations—but my hopes were dashed entirely. Not a single baby had had more than its napkin changed and some not even that! So they were all to wash and change and the mothers had to be tidied up and made comfortable and, hurry as I would, I did not finish until close upon 9.30. By that time, I was longing for supper and bed. Just as I was going upstairs to the Sister's room to report, another nurse ran past me and, when I got to the door, Sister looked up saying 'Ah, there is somebody already in her cloak and bonnet, take her. You don't mind going out again, do you, Nurse? It is a case of P.P.H. and somebody must go at once and the others have not come back from supper. Never mind your bag, one of the others can do that for you for once and you will want one of the big ones'. So, off we went.

Now P.P.H. is the 'Marie Celeste' nightmare and nobody would dream of delaying, even if it meant an indefinite postponement of bed and supper.

When we arrived at the house, we were taken upstairs to the patient's room. The people were Jews and rather more respectable than many we went to, as they had two fair-sized rooms and a kind of cupboard between them. The first room was where the patient was but, at first glance, we did not notice her, as the room was full of people. There was a large table, round which six men were sitting smoking and talking; three or four women were sitting or standing about the room, while the floor simply swarmed with crawling children and from the inner room came the sound of more voices and the reek of oily, Jewish cooking.

Our first action was to clear the room—all the men and most of the women and children we turned into the street. The husband, several children of varying ages and four women who had been in the inner room and claimed to be near relations we allowed to remain, on condition they kept the door shut between and only appeared if we asked for anything. Then we questioned the husband, to try and find out what was the matter and why it had happened. He told us, as if it was quite the usual and correct thing to happen, that, as soon as the nurses had left after the baby was born, some friends had come in to congratulate them and cheer his wife up. She had not felt very well, but had sat up and tried to entertain them and about half an hour later had started to bleed so violently that she had got frightened and had sent him to up to the Hospital for the Nurse to come, and their friends had stopped to keep her company till we returned.

Meanwhile, we had been inspecting the woman and demanding boiling water and various other necessaries; we then turned him out and set to work, but our efforts were of no avail and at last we had to send for the Sister and the J.R.A., who turned up almost immediately, as they had been expecting us to send, and were quite ready to start. While Nurse and I were there by ourselves we had found it quite difficult to keep the people in the next room and the door shut but, when the Doctor arrived, it seemed an absolute impossibility, until we tied the two door handles together so that, if one opened one door, it slammed the other, so that we managed to get some privacy, without entirely cutting ourselves off from our hot water supply, which was in the further room, The outer door was locked. At last, having successfully accomplished what we had set out to do, we departed to beds and baths. It was about 2 a.m. when I got to mine and I thanked my lucky stars that I was allowed to sleep peacefully till morning and even have my breakfast and wash my nine district babies without interruption.

'No, Sister, I don't know what to do with him.
He is so mimicky with his food at home'.

* * * * *

'You find it difficult to live on what you get?
Then why don't you raise your charges a little?'.

'Raise my charges! Never! I'd never raise my charges
on the Indignant Poor!'.

AN IMPRESSION

There is something curiously exciting in one's return to London by night after a long absence, but there are comparatively few who are able to enjoy the sensation to the full; the mystery and enchantment are lost in the short drive in a taxi to a respectable home, club or hotel that one knows well. There is only one other place that has raised the same kind of feeling of excited anticipation and mysterious pleasure in me—Venice! I came to it too by night, in inky darkness and coming out from the station to the broad flight of steps that lead down to the Grand Canal all was strange—it was like taking one's first plunge in the vast unknown. The unfamiliar cries, the splash of the water and the lights from the gondolas and reflections—sudden shapes looming up out of the darkness and disappearing again as suddenly—the soft motion of the gondola as one pushed off and glided away into the dark masses of buildings and narrow waterways that opened suddenly before one, the lighted windows above and lanterns on the guiding posts. This was no ordinary world one had come to—where would one's way lead and what would one find when one arrived? This night in London was the same—I had been away for some months and was making my way from somewhere in the region of Victoria—eastward. Oxford Street was under repair so the old bus lurched and swung along the side streets. At nine o'clock or rather after, all that part of London is very quiet—the pleasure seekers are already away and the workers for the most part have gone home, so on we swung, getting back to the main thoroughfare from Bloomsbury, the change from the dim light to the brilliant arch lights stretching like a golden serpent east and west overhead was very striking but it was not here that the real mystery and excitement began.

Charging and lurching along it seemed at a tremendous pace, through Holborn, Newgate, past St Pauls, a dim mass on one's right—up Cheapside past the Bank, Cornhill, Leadenhall Street to Aldgate Pump. Here quite suddenly the entire character of the place changes, the road widens and people appear in masses along either side of the road—many lights at irregular intervals are seen, some high, some low, some dancing and floating along the road, but none are bright enough to dispel the gloom that hangs over everything. People, thousands of them, all it seems intent on moving but all so closely packed on the pavements that they look like a slow dark stream rather than many individuals with separate existences and wills of their own. For a moment, though, one realises their individuality as one passes a street corner and there under a lamp stands a man perched above the crowd that has collected round him while he lifts up his voice and waves his arms. Two policemen stand at the edge of the crowd apparently quite oblivious to what is going on so close beside them.

What can that man have been propounding with so much fervour [*sic*] and energy? Was it the Gospel of Christ he was preaching to the poor and lowly? Was that why the policemen looked so unconcerned? Far more likely he was telling the 'poor in spirit' that 'Red Revolution' was the only cure for their ills and that the only way for them to arrive at happiness and success was to walk through the blood of their oppressors. The police will let them talk so long as it ends there. They say that talk gets rid of a lot of hot air and helps to ventilate the district. Another flash at a street corner shows a winkle stall driving a thriving trade. Old Mrs Winkle has a kind and cheery face and a broad Irish accent. She slipped on the wet curb while carrying a bucket of water and winkles a few months ago and broke her ankle and was taken into hospital. At first when asked her occupation all she would own to was that she was 'something in the fish trade' as she thought it sounded 'common' to say she kept a winkle stall!—but later she owned up when she found that there was another Mrs Winkle in the same ward and no one thought disparagingly of her occupation. She is a happy soul and always makes the best of every situation. She recovered and returned to her corner stall in a remarkably short time and now we only get a passing glimpse as our snorting monster rushes on.

Strange cries come out of the darkness and flares as we pass a row of stalls, then a brilliantly lighted house of entertainment with the usual crowds hanging about the doors. Another side street out of which comes the sound of music and a glimpse of little flying, hopping, dancing figures—a red glow at another corner and a delicious smell of roasted chestnuts. There is something wild and energetic and eager for life in the atmosphere—uncertainty and anticipation of adventure are in the swing of the bus, the still half-dimmed lights above one's head, the brighter dancing ones below, and the dark shifting masses of humanity, the huge trams and lorries, the hoots of the cars and cries of the people all grip one—on, on, one know [sic] not where the road may lead or to what adventure until one pulls up with a jolt at the curb and the conductor yells 'London 'Orspital'—one's journey is ended and one is back in all the old familiar noise and dirt—'give us a aipenny laidy'—'Garn she ain't no laidy—she's a nurse'—and so to Matron's office—orders for tomorrow? 'No, nurse, you must catch the midnight train from Euston, it is most important—I am glad you did not stay out any later—would you like any help? The taxi is ordered and here are the 'mackintoshes'. 'Thank you Sister, I have had supper'.

The adventure!—but how different from anything one has imagined—another rush through the dark to end perhaps in a tussle between life and death, the advent of a new life, or a passing knell.

* * * * *

PRIVATE STAFF

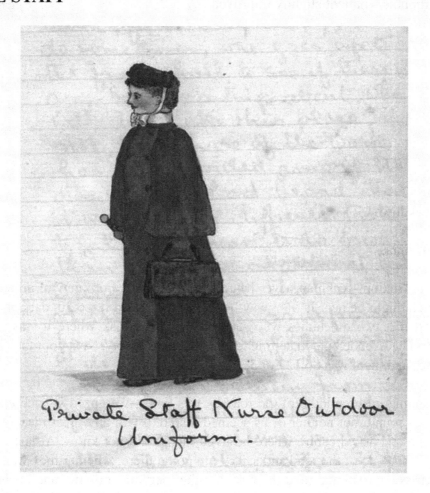

Private Staff Nurse Outdoor Uniform.

Case 1

H.B.—Age 76
Diabetes—Senile Decay etc.

No treatment.

Went to call on the village schoolmaster—buried three wives and drinks—offered me as a suitable 4th.

Gas fitter in the house—married man, offered me as a capable and sensible young woman— suitable as a second if he wanted one.

Was also offered to the barber and the local publican.

Very disturbed because when patient tried bellowing like a bull and screaming at the top of his voice I only smiled at him and asked him to do it again instead of getting frightened or annoyed. He did not trouble to do it again.

Stayed two months—patient slightly improved.

Case 2

Mrs. J.—Maternity

Case 3

Mr. M—Age 62
Nervous Breakdown

Rest Cure—2 nurses.

Arrived at . . . Station—cabman never heard of *The Avenue*, but knew of all sorts of other avenues which might be near it—anyway he would try to find it—6.30, dark and no people about. At last met two old ladies who stopped the cab to ask where it was going. They directed us to The Avenue but, on getting to No. 23, it was empty. Next door they had no need for any nurses and there was no 123 or 32.

We were standing in the middle of the road by this time—we gazed at each other, the cab and the houses round, but neither of us seemed inspired with any great idea. We knew the Doctor's name and asked cabby where he lived but he did not know. At last I turned to a house at the other side of the road and said 'I am going there, whether they want me or not' and went across the road and rang the bell. A rather nervous looking man opened the door and I remarked cheerfully 'You are expecting two nurses, aren't you?' to which he replied 'Oh, yes, at least I think Mrs M. was expecting them, only the Doctor is not here'. I suggested that the doctor did not matter so much as long as the patient was to be found, so he asked us to come into the drawing room and begged us to sit down and he would tell the mistress.

We waited nearly half an hour. The room was small and filled to overflowing with very much upholstered furniture, looking glasses, gorgeous vases, dried grasses and sham flowers and wool mats. At last a little and oldish lady came in. She was dressed in a very stuffy red and black dress and looked almost as much upholstered as her chairs. Her hair was very greasy and brushed flat back from her forehead and there was a large comb at the back. She came right into the room and shut the door with an air of mystery before she spoke, then without even saying 'How do you do' she announced that it was quite impossible for either of us to go up and see the patient and what was more we must be very quiet as he was not to know we were in the house. She did not dare introduce us, but we must wait until the Doctor came, he would do it. She then departed and left us again, with permission to sit down until the Doctor came. We waited for about another hour and a half and then at last the Doctor came. He said he would take whichever of us was to be the Night Nurse up and introduce the patient. The night work fell to me and I was taken up expecting a really violent scene, but when I was admitted I only found a very mild old gentleman, who melted into tears at intervals throughout the evening.

That night I found it very difficult to keep awake, as I had been up since 6 a.m. and I had to sit in a very dim and uncertain light and keep absolutely still and silent as the least movement roused my patient as he slept very lightly. In the morning I suggested that I should wash him, but he flatly declined to allow himself to be touched. After some persuasion, though, I managed to get him to wash his own hands and face, standing in his pyjamas by his bed, as he absolutely refused even to try to wash *in* bed. Then in came 'The Mistress' in a state of semi undress. She had had orders from the Doctor that if she went into her husband's room she must *not* talk business and she must be cheerful, so she came to side of the bed, leaning a little forward, planted her fists about a yard apart on its edge, gazed at him and grinned. This lasted fully a minute; at last I asked about Mr M.'s breakfast and when would be the best time to do the room. I was told the time for breakfast and that I might do the room before that. I said very well, if I was supplied with the necessary implements I certainly would, only could the maid just come and do the grate first as it would make rather a dust. 'The Mistress' look [sic] horrified. Mr M. would not possibly have the servants in while he was in bed—he would object and that would disturb him so. So I said 'Oh very well let me have the things and I will do it then but they must be brought up to the door because the Doctor's orders were that I was not to leave the room'.

Up the things came and I set to work; the room was quite disgusting and the white paint, of which there seemed an unreasonable quantity, filthy—so I washed it, a bit every day until I got all round it. There was a marvellous collection of half used patent medicines and powders for sleeplessness: the latter I pocketed until I could ask the Doctor if he knew of their existence. I also secreted all the razors and scissors I could find as one does hear of suicidal tendency in people who suffer from melancholia, especially if they are in the habit of taking drugs which Mr M. seemed to be from the number of bottles and powders I had found about.

Breakfast came next and I hardly knew how to keep awake, as I had been up since 6 a.m. the day before and in a very busy ward, but I comforted myself with the thought that the Doctor would soon arrive—he said he would come early, as he wanted me to stay on duty until he came as he was to introduce the second nurse. Mrs M. tried to be cheerful every time she came in, in her peculiar way, and the morning wore on. Dinner time came and no Doctor. Mrs M. expressed her sympathy and said I must be sleepy after being up all night with nothing to do; wouldn't I like to clean the silver on her dressing table the following night? She had any quantity of it and it needed cleaning badly but I declined with thanks as my patient slept little enough as it was and would probably do so not at all if I did that, as I would have to have a good deal more light than he would care for and make a certain amount of noise.

After dinner Mr M. proceeded to tell me all about the business and family troubles that had been brought about by his son and which had caused his illness and absolute ruin. The ruin was not nearly so absolute as he imagined, but to think it was, was bad enough poor man. He finished up by saying that he did not know how we thought he was going to pay two nurses. I felt a little surprised and asked how he knew there were two, as his wife and I were the only people who had come near him and it turned out that Mrs M. had told him. At about 2 p.m. the Doctor came with no explanation or apology for his lateness and I retired to bed and to sleep until about 1 a.m. when I came on duty again. In the morning, while I was doing the room, in came Mrs M. with her usual 'cheerful' expression. I just went to the door to fetch something in and turned back rather suddenly to find her whispering to him. The minute she saw me turn she stopped. The next time I went to the door I stopped before I put my head out and reminded her that there was to be no business talked and she hurriedly assured me that she remembered quite well and would not dream of it. The coal was just out of reach so I had to go a step or two away from the door and as I returned I heard her distinctly saying something about the money matters she had been forbidden to mention. I was really angry with her and told her so and also said that if she could not obey orders she would not be allowed to come into the room, at which she flared up in a fearful passion and wondered what the world was coming to if a wife could not say what she liked to her husband and was to be turned out of his room. She would *not* stay out, she would come in whenever she liked etc. etc.

I let her finish what she had to say and then told her she would do nothing of the sort without the Doctor's permission while I was on duty and she would not get that if she insisted on trying to talk business every time I turned my back. At this she subsided and went out of the room and did not return again until I went off duty—but she got permission from the Doctor to come in and out as she liked. He said it was not worthwhile trying to stop her.

Next morning I was busy at the far end of the room when she came in just before breakfast and I suppose she thought I would not notice her because she began whispering at once about a letter she had got on some of these wretched business matters, so I got up and said 'Now Mrs M., no business'. She turned nearly purple in the face and said 'Oh no, no, really I did not mention *anything*. I was only reassuring and setting his mind at rest'. I told her it was no use pretending as I had heard what she said and she was not going to do it. Also that it was no earthly use our trying or the Doctors going on so, if his orders were not carried out and we were not allowed to do our duty. Again she flared up and protested that she did not believe in Doctors, they knew nothing, they did not understand her husband, she had known him much longer than they had and ought to know more about him, that she never had believed in them and never would, so I asked her why she had sent for the Doctors at all if she knew so much better than they did—then she departed.

I used to go down and have breakfast with her first while the other nurse stayed with Mr M. and as soon as I returned she used to go down to hers. This morning when I went down Mrs M. beamed on me and said 'Good morning'. I wondered what had happened as she had only left me five minutes before in a distinctly bad temper. Then she began 'I have had some fresh news about our business today' and proceeded to tell me all that I had heard her telling her husband just before and finished up by saying 'but you will be careful not to mention it to him won't you—you see the Doctor says he is not to hear anything about any business matters'. I began to think there must be more the matter with the woman than the man. We nurses were certainly both tall and dark, but there the likeness ended—our faces were quite different also the other nurse had a broad Yorkshire accent and I am afraid I can't even put one on when I want to. She has a slight stoop and a 'rounded contour' while I have been described as 'going straight up and down like a yard of pump water'.

One thing that was a continual source of joy to us both was Mrs M.'s idea that anxiety about her husband had quite spoilt her appetite. What it can have been when it was not spoilt I don't know. When I arrived at a meal, breakfast for instance, she would sit at the head of the table and present me with a rasher of bacon, one pat of butter, one piece of toast, one cup of coffee and if I demanded it, one piece of bread. In turn she would help herself to the same only doubling the toast and butter, complaining the whole time of her lack of appetite. Nevertheless, she finished up everything before I went, then on nurse's appearance she would start again and exactly repeat the meal she had had with me, so that every time she got rather more than double what either of us had.

We only stayed a week and so we were not really starved; beside the servants sent us up plenty on our tray for the night and we shared a meal before Nurse went to bed, or I am afraid she might have been the worse for wear, as I seemed to be able to exist quite comfortably on much less than she could and she only got one meal more than I did in the 24 hours. At the end of four days the doctor said he was not going to bother any more, he could not do anything and nor could we if the 'old woman' would go on like that—she was sure to worry him to death in the end as she had her first husband and no power on earth would stop her. We were not too sorry to say goodbye, though it certainly had had its amusing side for us, but perhaps not for the patient.

Case 4

Mrs J.—Miscarriage 5 months

When I arrived all was over and there was only the tidying to be done. The Doctor was still there and a local Nurse who had been got in until I could arrive. My first impression was that the whole place was lined with looking glasses. I could turn nowhere without seeing myself at least twice over. Then the Doctor engaged my attention for a time and when he went away, I had the cleaning up to do. The Doctor had not gone downstairs many minutes when I noticed the patient was looking very queer and she complained of feeling faint and so, seeing the Doctor's carriage still at the door, I ran to tell him and ask what he would like to have done. He seemed greatly excited and came upstairs. As I came in again I remembered the looking glasses and tipped one up and turned another and left a cupboard door ajar to hide a third—because I thought that if the Doctor was going to do anything it was just as well for the patient not to see too much of what was going on behind her back. When the Doctor had gone, the patient turned to me and exclaimed in a plaintive sort of voice 'Nurse, why did you move the looking glasses, I could not see anything that was going on and I would like to have so much. The other nurse left them just as they were and I saw *everything*'.

Next morning when the Doctor came he entertained us at great length with an account of the Nurse he had had in. A very 'worthy woman' he said, but with a 'limp and a sniff' and not the most elementary ideas about surgical cleanliness. For instance, when he asked her to hand him some swabs, she first proceeded to wipe her nose with the back of her hand, then she took up the swabs in that hand and, seeing a spot of something on a chair close to her, wiped it up with the swabs before handing him them. Needless to say they were rejected. Every time the Doctor came he had some new and absurd thing to tell us about and invariably acted all the parts. He would have made a splendid rather low 'comedian' but for some reason or other had drifted into the medical profession, where at times he struck me as being rather trying.

I was only with Mr J. one week as they were not well off and so wanted somebody who would cook, do all the housework and washing, as well or instead of the nursing and so, as £2.2s.0d. a week was considered too much to give for a 'Char', I had to leave as soon as the Doctor could say that the patient was 'going on all right'.

Case 5

Mrs. F.—Maternity.

Mrs. F. was the wife of an American doctor who had come over to Europe to study special branches of his profession. When they had started over from America, Mrs. F had seemed a little seedy but it had not entered either of their heads what was the matter, but before they had been in England very long they discovered and then came a terrible hunt for suitable rooms and doctor and nurse, as Mrs. F. utterly refused to be taken home to America as she was sure her husband would never come back by himself and there was so much he had wanted to do and had not yet accomplished.

I was interviewed some weeks before the event was expected and was only telephoned for on the morning of the very day the baby arrived. She was a very small dark-eyed black-haired baby, which luckily pleased both parents. The day after, my troubles began. Mrs. F. felt so well she wanted to sit up and even to get out of bed and her husband did not see why she should not; it was the fashion in America, but I told them it was not in England and that in all probability the English doctor who was attending would not let her out of bed for three weeks at least.

Next came struggles over the baby's food. It would not take the breast for the simple reason that there was no milk, but nothing must do but that we must go on trying. The baby got thinner and thinner and her cry became weak and fretful. At last I became really frightened about the child and said I must start bottle-feeding her—she had lost weight and had that strange old glazed look about her eyes that only starving babies get and so at last the doctor gave his consent. The doctor wrote out a special prescription with amounts and hours of feeding and the alterations that were to be made from day to day. Very weak to start with, of course, but weak as it was after so long a period of starvation, her digestion was not capable of managing it, but we had to struggle on. The doctor said it must come right, his prescription for the food was scientifically correct and must be kept to. Meanwhile though the child had stopped losing weight in the way that it had done at first, she still was at a standstill and made no progress.

The first time I took her out I found that do what I would I could not keep her warm, she was so little and frail, so in the future I took her out lying on a hot water bottle in my arms, but the food was what troubled me most and then to add to the worry the father said he was sure it was all because we fed her too often and we had long discussions on the subject. I stuck to it that two hourly feeds were right for babies under a month and he said three hourly were quite sufficient. At last I had to tell him that I was working for an English doctor and two hours was considered long enough between an English baby's feeds, I intended to stick to what my English doctor said till either he told me differently or Dr. F. told him to go about his own business and took the case himself. Then he seemed to realise that I meant what I said and let me go on my own way unhindered.

The next event was that the English doctor fell ill and could not come and so sent a friend of his, a very bluff old fashioned old G.P. He came and heard what I had to say about the child and then looked at her and then grunted good deal and then remarked 'Humph, science, that is what is the matter with it. Put her back on plain unboiled milk and barley, whatever strength you find she can take and give her a good feed of bengers food every night'. From that moment the child revived and began to grow.

At the end of three weeks Dr. F. decided to go to Vienna to see the hospital there and so Mrs. F. and I were left to ourselves at the top of the house. Luckily for us there were no other boarders in the place just then, as there was only one wretched little maid who did practically all the work of a four-storied house with fires in the attics and no hot water laid on higher than the first floor, besides doing most of the cooking.

The landlady was the widow of an American Homeopathic Plymouth Brother and lived up to it all, but found taking in boarders a trial and a comedown after having been the wife of such a shining light. She would have been most entertaining to listen to if one had had more time, but as I did all that ever was done in our room and a half at the top of the house and carried up all the water (of which we used a most enormous quantity, as I not only washed the mother and baby, but also various of the baby's garments and portions of the room) and most of the coal and food so that there was not much time to spare. If one asked the way to some shop in the town, our landlady would keep one amused for twenty minutes or so with her vivid description of the roads and houses and shops on the way and her dramatic actions and attitudes, but one never carried away the least recollection of how to get there.

When I left, the baby had just regained its birth weight and Mrs. F. was very well, though rather nervous and miserable at being left to the tender mercies of the little maid and the landlady, and I often wondered how she managed to get through the week still left until her husband returned from Vienna.

Case 6

Mrs. B—Fibroids

My next case was a lady of about 45. When I arrived I was taken up to see my patient. I could hardly find her, she was almost smothered in a huge feather bed. The doctor was a very stout fatherly old man and on the second day when he came, hearing that I had not been out, he asked if I would put on my bonnet and come with him in his carriage. When I got back after about an hour's outing I found the whole household in a terrible state of mind; they were all quite sure the patient was going to die almost immediately and that the doctor had taken me out in his carriage to tell me so, not liking to do so in the house. Why I could never make out. I tried to assure them that it was not so, but all to no purpose.

When I had been there about a week my patient seemed no worse, but not much better, so they settled to have a specialist down from town and by some lucky chance one of our own men, Dr. Russell Andrews, was chosen. The doctor told me he had a great liking for 'Dicky' Andrews as he had been the first person to teach him any anatomy when he was quite a little boy and used to sit on his knee, but why he was called 'Russell' now or had been 'Dicky' when he first went to hospital he could never make out, as his name was 'Henry'.

Well, I was told that on a certain day Dr. Andrews would come and examine the patient and if there was any necessity for an operation he would come again another day and do it. For some unknown reason I thought I would have basins and lotions ready in case he wanted to do anything besides just examine and I also insisted on a smaller bed with an ordinary spring mattress being put up in the room as I told Mrs. B that I had not the face to let one of our own doctors to come and find me with a patient in a *feather* bed, that she *must* just, while she was being examined, get into the other bed. I also secreted a shutter under the spring, just to prevent them from bouncing while she was being examined and had a good many superfluous ornaments and pieces of furniture removed from the room.

When Dr. Andrews arrived the room was ready and the patient dressed in a most businesslike 'examination gown'. He only took about two minutes to make up his mind what he wanted to do as he had hardly started to examine her before he enquired whether there was a mackintosh in the bed, and on hearing that there was, I was sent to get out his instruments and steriliser and he would operate on the spot. Wasn't I thankful then that I had got basins and lotions and boiling water ready and could produce all that was wanted; also that I had not allowed my patient to stay in the large feather bed. All went well in spite of the rest of the household making up its mind with great determination that the patient was on the point of death for at least a fortnight, though I promised them faithfully that she was doing as well as it was possible for anybody to do and that she was recovering rapidly.

One peculiarity my patient had was that it invariably made her very ill to eat eggs in any form and as the doctor's one great cry was 'feed her up, feed her up, give her plenty of eggs, at least two a day', this peculiarity became a nuisance and I began to wonder if it was a fact or an idea and decided to experiment. First I tried beating up an egg in milk and giving it to her to drink out of a feeder so that she could not see the colour and as that had no evil effect I got bolder and had eggs put in her puddings and soups. Also I had custards made with Bovril and they all went down and she throve [*sic*] upon them and never found it out, until one evening I left the mixing of the egg and milk to her sister who was staying there and she chose a very highly coloured egg and I think cannot have mixed it very thoroughly as the patient noticed something peculiar and turned her feeder round and looked inside and, of course, saw it was not just ordinary milk and had to be told what we had been doing. Luckily she was nearly well by that time and it did not matter much if she did stop her eggs as she could take anything else she liked instead. She had recovered remarkably quickly, but always declared that she would have got well 'much quicker' if it had not been for all those eggs I had given her.

Case 7

Post-influenza and pneumonia

The next case I went to was an elderly man who had had influenza and pneumonia, but was getting better. He had two nurses but one of them had been booked for a special case sometime earlier and so could not stay with him more than six weeks and I had to go to take her place. I was told in the Office that they were very difficult people and I would need all the tact I had. They had been very rude to Matron about the change of nurses and were quite prepared to thoroughly dislike anybody who took the place of the first nurse, whom they said they liked.

The journey down seemed interminable as I was sent off by a very slow train so as to arrive at the exact moment when required. When I got to the station (Torquay) I found there was only a very limited number of cabs and my porter and another nearly had a stand up fight over the last one, but the catastrophy was averted by the suggestion that we might share a cab between us, so I and some very jovial trippers all got in together and I dropped the trippers part of the way up the first hill and so went on by myself. The nurse who was there already was on day so after being introduced to the patient and his relations I went to bed.

He was quite a nice old man with an aversion to being washed and an idea that if every spot of soap was not rinsed off before he was dried he would go rotten. This was rather a bother as often when I had quite finished and was putting him into his clothes, he would suddenly think he remembered seeing a spot of soap on his arm and leg and we had to begin all over again with the rinsing and drying process.

The wife and daughter were the most forbidding looking couple and the son simply silly. Soon after I arrived I discovered large notices stuck in all the bookshelves—'Books not to be removed from this shelf'—and wondered what was the matter with the books. One day I was reading a book of my own as I sat in the dressing room next door to my patient, when his daughter came in, glared at me and demanded what I was reading. I told her and she exclaimed with horror 'Oh, I don't think you must read that—I am sure my father would not like it'. I told her I was sorry but what I read was my own concern and nothing to do with her or her father, especially as the book never so much as went into his room, but I offered to cover it with brown paper if she did not like the look of its cover. It was a history of the Indian Mutiny—which I did.

Another thing that came to be annoying at times was her habit of popping in and out in the middle of the night to see if I was awake and suggested that I should do this or that part of his treatment, all at the wrong times and generally about ten to twenty minutes after I had finished doing them. It used to be 'Don't you think his poultice needs changing or don't you think he could take a little nourishment or hadn't the window better be closed or opened'— but what annoyed me more than anything else was one night after I had gone through the usual performance of promising to call them for anything—the daughter heard him cough a little and jumped up and ran and called first her mother, then her brother and without a word or sign to me they all three slipped into the patient's room, through the further door and before I knew what they were up to, they were playing at death bed scenes all round the poor old man, who was really rather better, but was nearly frightened out of his wits, because he thought I had sent for his family and so he must be much worse and it was only with great difficulty that I got the three of them out of the room and locked the door so that in the future they always had to come through my room to get to him. I was angry with them and next morning they knew it. It had taken me nearly all the rest of the night to get the poor old fellow quiet and happy again. When he was well enough to move we left Torquay and went to his son-in-law's house near Hungerford—there the day nurse left us.

I was still to remain on night duty while his family looked after him in the daytime. They assured me that it was quite all right as they had nursed him through several illnesses before and thoroughly understood what to do—so I went to bed—telling them if they needed anything or got into difficulty, they must call me. I was kept awake for a long time that afternoon by a tremendous thunderstorm, but just as it began to get dark the storm cleared and I began to doze, when suddenly there was a tremendous rattle at my door and in came the daughter, a woman of 40, with a medicine bottle in her hand—'Oh, nurse the label on this bottle says a 6th part to be taken every 4 hours—how do I know what a 6th part is?'. I explained and lay down again—I was just dropping off a second time when there was another rattle and in she came again with another bottle—'this bottle has an 8th part every 6 hours on its label, do I measure that the same way—you see this is an 8th and the other was a 6th so you see I did not know'. I sat up and explained again and told her that it would not hurt anybody to drink the whole of that bottle full right off as it was very mild, but the other one she must be careful about as it was stronger. When I got up I found she had been giving him double doses of the strong medicine and half doses of the milder kind and she had nursed him in several severe illnesses before. He must have been a very tough old man when she started.

After that I was left in peace as I only saw the family for a few minutes at night when I got up and again for a little while in the morning when the doctor was there and before I went off duty. For the rest I fed in a room by myself and wandered over the country until it was time to go to bed, finding butterfly orchids and other treasures in the woods and fields that the others never saw or dreamed of even. One day I met them on my way home with a large bunch of various kinds of flowers. They looked at me in surprise and enquired what I was going to do

102

with all those queer things and where I could have been. They never saw them along the sides of the roads when they went out walking.

At other times I went to the kennels belonging to the house and played with the hound pups, there were swarms of them, or the stables to see the horses. The nurse who followed me did not like the country and confessed to me that she had cried herself to sleep many an afternoon from sheer loneliness because the 'family' never spoke to her.

Case 8

Slight concussion and shock after a mild motor accident

My patient was a lady of about 35 who 'moved in the very highest circles'. In fact she claimed Princess Victoria as one of her personal friends and Princess Royal came to enquire and brought her children. The Earl of Athol visited her and another titled gentleman from the North, who owned coal, came to see her and I had to be brought in and shown off to them all.

The first time Princess Victoria came and I was sent for I had not the least idea who she was and stalked into the room with a broad grin and shook hands exclaiming with pleasure over some lovely flowers she had brought. Then my patient told me who she was and I was so overcome with shyness that I seized upon the flowers, ostensibly to put them in water and bolted from the room with the result that the Princess was reported to say that if she was ever ill she hoped she would have that nurse.

The amount of scandal I listened to, past, present and future, about everybody notable in every walk of life was wonderful, but it all seems to have slithered in at one ear and out at the other or at any rate most of it has and I can't remember more than half a dozen names out of all the scores I heard while I was there.

After about a week in Town it was thought advisable to take my patient to the Country, so we were invited to a house her sister had taken at Ascot and we were to go part of the way by motor to get her used to it again and I was very glad when that journey was over as my arm was nearly black and blue where she gripped it every time we passed anything or turned a corner.

I had not been near Ascot since I was about 6 or 7 and did not expect to remember it much, but I soon found I recognised first one thing, then another and even remembered my way about fairly well, only most of the distances seemed short. I had very little to do besides amuse myself and so used to go for long walks, my patient being practically well. One day I was out and got to some boggy land; I was jumping from tuft to tuft when one gave way under me and I slipped and twisted my ankle over. It was awfully painful and for a few minutes I could not stand on it, so I took off my shoe and stocking and dangled my foot in the stream that ran close by, then having tied my ankle up with my handkerchief, I managed to hobble home where I bandaged it properly. I helped my patient to bed as usual that night standing on one leg as much as I could and then went to bed myself.

Suddenly in the middle of the night the electric bell went off just under my bed and I bounced out not thinking of my foot until it touched the floor then I nearly sat down on top of it and just managed to crawl into the next room, thinking something awful must have happened to my patient and feeling very sick with the pain in my foot. When I got there, there was nothing the matter. Oh no, only she was awake and thought I might like to know. Did she want anything. No, only she was awake that was all. Quite comfortable. Yes. Which was more than could be said for me, so I went back to bed until morning. When I got back to Hospital a week later my ankle was much better, but I was sent to the sick room for ten days and then was sent about with convalescent children because regular ward work would have been too trying until my ankle got a bit stronger. Then about a fortnight later I went off to my ninth case.

There was one thing that up until about this time nobody had been able to explain that now came to light and that was the disappearance of certain sums of money, among them the £1 from the ward I had been in about a year back. Since then no more had been taken from the wards, but a good many small sums had been missed from locked cupboards and drawers in the nurses' quarters and at last Matron and the Committee had thought it wise to employ detectives to try and discover where and how the money went. They watched most carefully for some time but the thief was so cunning that still the money went and the detectives got no clue whatever until at last they tried laying traps by leaving purses with marked coins in them in places easy of access. The coins were not only marked but had a kind of colouring matter put on them which when dry could not be seen, but no sooner was it made damp then whatever it touched was stained a bluish colour. Presently a certain nurse's towels and pocket handkerchiefs were noticed by the Laundry Sister and it was reported and she was watched most carefully. At last, one day after a purse with marked money in it had disappeared the blue mark was noticed on her hands and she was sent for to Matron's office and accused before her and the Chairman. At first she denied all knowledge of what they were talking about. Then the priest of her church came and interviewed her (she was a very high church Christian) and at last she confessed it all to him. She had taken the money with no other object than to be able to give presents to her fellow nurses and Sisters she admired. Not a penny of it went home though her poor old mother was very badly off and another sister of hers, who was not earning nearly as much as she did, sent regular sums home every quarter to help keep the home together.

This we learnt from the poor old mother who was sent for and came nearly broken hearted. She had so hoped her eldest daughter was getting on better now, she had had trouble with her right along until she had come to the Hospital and even finished her four years without any mishap, but this was worse than any of her other misdeeds. Matron was so sorry for the poor woman that she promised she would try not to have the daughter set to prison even for the night before the trial—so she got the police to leave her in the sick room and there for two days and a night she was kept entirely in bed with a special nurse all the time to see that she did not run away. She was remanded in court and was to be watched and brought up for trial and imprisonment any time within the next two years if found offending again and with that her mother took her home and I have heard no more of her.

Case 9

Next for me came a baby case and then one day I was told that one of our surgeons was going to do an operation on a small boy for tonsils and adenoids or P.N.G.'s as we call them. I was to take all that would be wanted and be there by 9.30 a.m. so as to be ready when he came. I was only to stay the day so I only needed to take a bag with mackintoshes, sponges, bowls etc. so off I went.

Case 10

I arrived at the station armed with everything I needed from the address to clean apron and collar to put on after the operation in case mine got soiled. I asked the way and, finding it was not far and I had plenty of time, thought I would walk to the house. When I got there and asked if Mrs. R was in, the maid with great surprise told me she did not live there and so I asked who did then and was she by any chance expecting a nurse. 'No' and her name was not one that could possibly be taken for the one I asked for.

Then I set to work and took all the addresses with any sort of family likeness to the one I had been given and tried to find a Mrs. R who lived anywhere near but with no result. As soon as the shops began to open I enquired there, then I found one that let me telephone to the Hospital to ask them if I had the address as they had given it. The one I had was the one given to them and they could offer me no help, but meanwhile the shopkeeper, being an intelligent man, had brought out a directory and was hunting through it and at last came upon the right name in a road without even the remotest connection to the one in the original address, so as a last resort, I had tried all the other Mrs. R's in the neighbourhood, I went there and at 11 a.m. instead of 9.30 a.m. I turned up.

Mrs. R. herself was out and the 2 boys were left in charge of a very kind but youthful nursemaid. Luckily the doctor was not coming until 12 so I had plenty of time to get things ready. When I had got all I wanted, the nursemaid said she would take the elder boy for a walk and leave me with the younger one. Mrs. R. generally came in to lunch, but she was not going to today—in fact she did not mean to come back until late in the afternoon when everything would be over. Everything went off quite satisfactory and when Mrs. R. did come in she paid the fee and offered me half a crown for my trouble, but she did not seem to have worried about her son in the very least. Her only anxiety was to go out again as soon as possible.

Case 11

Lady B.
Tenotomy of a Ductorlongus [*sic*] [an operation on the adductor longus tendon!]

This was a big house in Park Lane and there were to be 2 nurses. We were shown into a large room that opened off our patient's and supposed that the operation would be there to save disturbing her, but we were told 'no' she wished it to be in her own room and she would have none of the furniture moved, so we had to wait until next morning before we could get anything arranged. In the meantime we collected all the necessary tables, bowls, jugs etc. and stacked them in the outer room which was to be our sitting room. Then the patient's husband came in, in a great state of agitation to ask if we really advised the operation, did we think it necessary and would it prove a success.

We happened not to have been told anything about it but did our best to soothe the poor man who was talking as if he had prepared a long speech to last an hour and a half and now found he would have to get it all in, in three quarters. When at last he stopped he was nearly breathless but not quite, having just enough left to tell us that we had not convinced him of the necessity for the operation nor that it would be useless, so he was going then and there, at 10 o'clock at night, to consult an eminent surgeon on the subject and off he went and we saw no more of him that night.

I was to be Night Nurse, but we could do nothing until the morning and our patient did not need us, so after making her acquaintance we both went to bed. I was taken right to the top of the house as it was thought to be the quietest place in the daytime, but I soon began to wonder what the rest of the house must be like. The room was small and contained a little narrow bed, a table, a chair and a wash stand and the window was small and round and the weather was hot, so I lent and opened my porthole, for that is what it was like, and the whole room more like a cabin than an ordinary bedroom. As I opened it a roar came in like a great sea, broken at frequent intervals by shrieks of motor horns and whistles. All the time I was there I used to wake up at intervals during the afternoon and evening and catching sight of my porthole and hearing the roar of traffic and wonder where I was and how it was that I was on a ship at sea.

Next morning we were up betimes and sent our patient to have her bath while we did what we could to get the room in order. We had not much time to waste as the operation was to be at 9.30 a.m., but between us we just managed to get the patient and the room as ready as possible under the circumstances before the surgeon and anaesthetist arrived, then much to everybody's surprise just as were about to begin the door opened and in walked one of our own Hospital visiting staff. Nurse and I were delighted to see him but I don't know if anybody else was. He explained that the night before the husband had come round to see him and seemed rather disturbed so he had promised to look in and see him in the morning and since he was here he thought it would be interesting 'just as a friend you know' to come and lend a hand with anything that was going—for his own 'amusement and instruction nothing else you know' and so on, so he came and helped and we were very pleased. The other surgeon draped his head in a wisp of gauze to try and make himself aseptic, but the gauze would not stay where it was and so was no earthly use to anybody and only a nuisance to him, making him very hot and uncomfortable. He offered another piece to our 'Tommy' but he refused with thanks—the other man eyed him critically and then asked if he considered oil for his hair a sufficient precaution as he looked at his well brushed head. Our Tommy growled 'No, I wash—clean water is good enough—soap and water,—and turned away to scrub his hands.

The anaesthetist had been fussing over first one thing and then another ever since he came, when it was not hairpins or teeth, it was the temperature of the room or the position of the patient's head, but at last we all got settled. The operation over, the anaesthetist hurriedly left his seat and darted across to the bed, which we had kept carefully covered, with hot water bottles inside and a slightly warm water pillow. He turned back the bedclothes and laid savage hands upon the hot bottles flinging them on the floor in his anxiety. I could not think what he was up to so I carefully picked them up and put them in again, then I saw he was trying to get at the water pillow and remove that, so I gently insinuated that he should leave it alone, then he explained himself.

He was afraid the patient might get burnt by the bottles before she came round from the anaesthetic. He had known of such cases where the nurses were careless so he made a point of always removing the hot bottles himself before the patient was put into the bed. I told him we were not careless and that there was no danger of our allowing our patient to burn herself.

Then his eye fell on one of the bottles I had replaced and thinking he had missed it in his first raid he seized it and threw it on the floor. All this time our 'Tommy' had been looking on with a smile and when he saw me pick the bottle up again and slip it into the bed as I covered the patient with a warm blanket he winked and nodded and whispered in a very stage whisper 'That's right nurse' before turning to the anaesthetist and trying to distract his attention.

Being Night Nurse I soon went off duty and to bed. When I came on duty again I was advised to lock the door from my patient's room into the passage and only keep the one from the dressing room, where I was to sit, open as my patient's husband never went to bed, but spent the night wandering from room to room and from chair or couch to couch there was one arranged for him in every room so that he could spend half an hour or so in each and nurse was afraid he might forget that his wife had just had an operation and wander into her room and disturb her just as she was going off to sleep. Nothing special happened for the first night or two except that I now and again met his 'Lordship' straying about with his arms full of great books when I went out to fetch anything and he informed me quite seriously that he <u>never</u> slept at all in the night, until one night as I was sitting quietly in my room I heard a tremendous crash and ran out to see what was the matter. There was a light in the drawing room, but no sound, so I went along and there sprawling at ease in the most comfortable chair with the electric light hardly 3 feet from his nose, was the precious man sound asleep and the floor all about him was strewn with the books he had been carrying. I turned out the light and went away leaving him to sleep and I heard no more until morning.

Very soon 'My lady' as Nurse persisted in calling her or 'Your Ladyship' instead of a simple 'You' or 'Lady . . . ', began to feel very much better and the first intimation of this I had was that on going on duty one night I found her hair strained back from her face and tied with an enormous light blue ribbon and curlers in the front. To add to this she asked for some sticking plaster which she proceeded to fasten her mouth with to keep it shut while she was asleep—the oddity of the result on her looks was very nearly too much for me and I was glad when I was able to turn out the light and leave her.

On the 10th day the stitches were to come out and nurse and I had a great boiling of instruments and making of lotions and spreading of towels preparatory to the arrival of the surgeon. He came and hardly more than glanced at the nail brush and soap we had put out for him to 'scrub up' with, then taking the dirty dressings in his hands examined them and deposited them in the bed. Nurse handed him a bowl of lotion with the instruments in it. He looked a little disconcerted, took them out and wiped them on the old dressing that was still in the bed and then proceeded to remove the stitches. Then I offered him some sterile dressings we had kept after the operation but he would use none of them, but fished in his bag for a little bit of crumpled gauze which he used. Luckily the wound was safely healed before he started or I do not know what the consequences might not have been.

Case 12

My next job was to take the place of a nurse for one night only. She was on 'night duty' and was wanted to go in for her C.M.B. exam and it was necessary to relieve her so that she might have a little rest beforehand.

The experience was unique! I went on duty to find the room in the most wonderful state of litter—I may say the permanent day nurse was not a Londoner—little scraps of cotton wool here, there and everywhere, dirty wine and medicine glasses, spoons and medicine bottles, brandy, jelly and lotions on every available flat surface, no method in this madness nor order anywhere so far as I could see. I was greeted faintly from the bed and only saw a hurrying vision departing from a further door, which was the day nurse. I was left in the midst of chaos with no official instructions to go upon, but I was not left long in doubt as to what would be wanted of me.

'I think I had better have just a teaspoonful of brandy now nurse'. I looked round wondering where or which of the many bottles it would be in. 'Over there on the dressing table and the spoon is on the wash stand. Yes the water out of the kettle and then in about ten minutes it will be time for my medicine'. The brandy was taken and the medicine found and by the time I had collected all the dirty glasses and washed them it was time to take the medicine and wash that glass. 'It is about time for me to take a little nourishment, I think I had better have a teaspoonful of Brands Essence and then it will be time for my pill in ten minutes and so we went on—never more than ten minutes interval and often not so long until midnight, then I was told to go into the next room and have my meal which was put in there—a raw egg, bread and butter and everything for making tea. 'Very nice', you say, but when all has to be done, the egg cooked, the kettle boiled and the tea made and everything disposed of within ten minutes, you would be a little doubtful I think.

I had left the Hospital about 8 p.m. having supped before that and was not having another chance of bite or sup until after 9 a.m. next day. However, it was only one night—if I had had to come again I would have stored my pockets with easily demolished eatables and could have taken a 'little nourishment' as often as my patient if I had so wished. After my meal we did the round of ten minute stunts again, then just for a change, a little rest was suggested but she could not sleep as she was, the bedclothes were far too heavy so I must take them all off and wrap each limb up separately in a small shetland shawl, her head could be on the pillow, but her feet must be placed on a chair and the central portion covered with a light blanket. When all this was arranged to her satisfaction, I was to get a chair and place it at a very uncomfortable angle by the bed and sit and fan her. Whatever happened I was not to stop for one single second as that second might be the very one at which she was just going to sleep and if I stopped at that critical point she might never manage to trap that elusive moment again. So I sat and fanned. For about three quarters of an hour she slept while my arm nearly dropped off as I had nothing to support it and I did not dare to move to another position or even rest as I was and I began to long for the ten minute changes again.

At last she woke and we started medicines, etc. until she suddenly thought of something we had not tried as yet. I was to wrap each finger and the thumb of her left hand in a narrow strip of white lint. Then I was to pull up an india rubber finger-stall over each. When that was done I was to see if the kettle was boiling and fetch a large enamel bowl, put it on the chair by the bed and she placed the tips of her fingers in the bowl while I was to pour boiling water from the kettle into the bowl until it came up to the first joints—she then waited for three minutes before taking her fingers out of the water, when they had to be undressed and wrapped up in fresh lint with ointment spread on the smooth side and the finger-stalls dried and replaced. This done she said she felt great relief and must now have a little nourishment.

Having had her nourishment she thought a compress on her arm would be nice if I could do exactly as she told me. There was a piece of flannel with a bit of oil-silk stitched on the back of it. This was to be placed in a cloth in the bowl we had just used and boiling water poured over it—it was then to be wrung out, opened and three drops from a certain bottle dropped upon the flannel. I was to take the flannel and lay it on my two hands held palm upwards—then clap suddenly and hard, re-open my hands and place the flannel on her arm and bandage in place. The whole was demonstrated to me and I obeyed orders exactly and was rewarded by being told that I had carried out her instructions better than anyone had ever done before.

About 7.30 a.m. I was told that as a great privilege, since I had done so well all night, I might be allowed to give my patient a little wash—a little indeed it proved to be. I collected water, towels, soap, sponge, etc. and was preparing to give her a real wash, but this was not the least bit what she meant. The towels were spread on the bed and the basin brought near but it was only arms as far as the elbows that had to be washed and the greatest horror was expressed when I started to dry them on a towel—that was far too rough—a silk pocket handkerchief was what was always used. Then her face—her nightgown had a high neck—two buttons to the collar—these I unfastened and started on the next, but with a terror struck voice my patient drew the nightgown collar together again with a 'you should not expose me so'. The wash ended at the chin and the elbows—there was no more done.

I was glad to go off duty and back to bed and Hospital after my strenuous night. I was also glad that although the dear lady asked for my name and address before I left and told me I was the most sympathetic nurse she had ever had I was never sent to her again. One could be sympathetic and even enjoy a night like that, a night but only one.

This lady has since died, probably of exhaustion—but I never heard how many of her nurses did the same.

* * * * *

After this I had a run of far less eventful cases. I see in looking through my books that there are two or three cases that I have left out that might be of interest and I propose to put them in here, although they will, of course, be out of the actual order in which they happened. The first is of no particular interest from a nursing point of view, but the House and grounds were extremely so. It was in Holland House and Lady I was my patient. It is a wonderful old house—it has a huge collection of most valuable things in it.

One night I was sitting in my room on night duty when about 2 a.m. I heard heavy, but quiet, footsteps coming along the passage. I wondered who it could be and thought perhaps somebody else was ill and they were coming to fetch me, but instead of coming to my door they went to the one opposite. I heard the door open and shut, quite quietly, and I wondered is it perhaps a thief come to take some of the valuables or a suffragette come to wantonly destroy, as one heard of them doing a good deal about that time. Anyhow who or whatever it was it had no business there at that time of night and I had better go and see, so up I got and went to the door and turned the light on in the passage. The handle on the door opposite was a hanging one and was still swinging as if it had only just been let go of. I opened the door and there was pitch darkness and no sound. I felt round for the electric light but could not find the switches and very little light shone in from the passage. I groped about a little but could find nothing and so went out again, shutting the door after me. I left the light in the passage and my door open so that I could see if anybody came out, and sat down to wait. Suddenly the two large folding doors burst open and knocked against the couch that I had pushed out of the middle of the room across them to get it out of the way. Nothing that I could see came through, but they banged shut again. I jumped up and ran to the other door and opened it but could hear nothing in the room and it was still too dark to see, so I closed the door and spent the rest of the night watching but nothing more happened.

When the housemaids came along I asked if everything was as usual in that room, if any window was open or draught that could have blown the doors open, but they said there was nothing to account for it and I heard no more. About a week later I met a fellow nurse who had once nursed there herself and as soon as she heard where I was she asked 'Oh, have you seen the ghost yet?'. That was the first I had heard of a ghost in the house, so I asked more about it and she told me that the last Lord Holland, who had lived in the time of the Charles' had had his head cut off and had lain in state at Holland House and ever since he had been walking about at night with his head under his arm. People generally met him on the floor below but sometimes he had been known to wander away from his usual beat. When I told nurse of what had happened the week before she was sure it must be he. Poor Lord Holland had not been able to settle which side to be on during the wars—his frequent changing of mind at last annoyed both sides so much that one or other made an end of his indecision or tried to. Perhaps he is still trying to make up his mind as he walks headless along the passage—but he left me in peace until just before I was leaving. I was then sleeping in the middle room instead of sitting up and woke up suddenly one night quite certain that somebody had just walked though my room into my patient's, so I jumped out of bed and followed but there was nobody to be seen either there nor in the passage beyond so I went back to bed and gave up ghost hunting.

Another skipped one was a baby in Ireland. My patient and her husband were both English. He was a retired soldier who had been deafened by gunfire—an extremely nice man who was devoted to the country and its ways. She was not devoted to any country and hated Ireland and the Irish.

I arrived on July 3rd and the baby put off coming until August 25th so I had a long wait, but they preferred to have me on the spot even for that length of time as we were a long way from the doctor and there was no telephone. The house was a large and comfortable country house with an extremely nice garden with a field in front that ran down to the river and a wood behind and fields all round. There was nothing for me to do so I spent my time rambling around the country and taking the dogs for walks and making friends with the cottage people round about. Mrs. C had a little fox terrier of her own and Major C had a pointer. The poor little fox terrier had a very dull time of it as Mrs. C had never thought of teaching it to come when called or do anything a proper dog should. She was afraid of it straying so she had a long wire stretched from one end of a path to the other and had the unfortunate dog fastened to it by a lead so that it could just run up and down the path but nothing more.

Her own daughter of about 3 she treated much in the same way. She had never in her life walked down the garden path without holding somebody's hand. She had only just begun to cross the room by herself if she wanted a toy. She was said to be 'so highly strung' that she got terrified by everything—a person in a hat would start her screaming until she lost control of herself all together and could not stop. She could never be taken to see an invalid aunt who lived just across the river because being in the boat frightened her so that she had one of her screaming fits. She could never be taken anywhere because the least change or new experience excited her so. I soon came to the conclusion that there was something wrong with the upbringing of both the dog and the child and thought I would try and see if I could make a change for one if not both and started on the dog. Soon we became firm friends.

When he had got to know me quite well I asked if I could borrow the pointer and take them both out for walks so that the well trained obedient dog could explain life to the other and teach him how he should behave. This worked splendidly and I soon was able to dispense with the tutor dog and take the pupil by himself. There was only one thing that was really too much for his feelings and tempted him beyond what seemed to him reasonable and that was *cows*. I tried scolding and persuading and at last had to lead him through fields where there were cows. He knew quite well he should not but he always felt he must chase them. Gradually he seemed to take less interest in them until one day I thought I would try again and let him run loose through a field where they were. The first field was all right, but the second was too much and off he went. I called and scolded and at last he came after a long race round and a stampede of cattle. I caught him by the collar and gave him two sound slaps, the first I had ever done, he wriggled out of my hands and rushed straight into the river and was not even attempting to swim, so there was nothing for it and I had to go in after him and fish him out. Luckily the river was not too deep there and we both got safely to shore with nothing worse than a wetting, but I never dared to hit the dog again.

Another day when I had scolded him more than he liked he ran away and hid and we never found him for two days. Then he was brought back by a neighbour who said he had been hiding in one of his barns all the time. You see I was the only person who had ever spoken to him as if he were a sensible creature, or took him out, so I suppose he thought life would not be worth living if I got cross and turned against him.

The child was the next thing, but I could not quite see how to start on her as long as her own Nanny was about, but presently I found she was leaving as she could not bear the idea of a new baby and an aunt was coming over to lend a hand until a new one could be properly established. After a day or two Auntie was quite ready to hand the child over to me for part of the day, so I got my chance. First I took her in the kitchen garden where I knew there were a lot of semi wild strawberries along the edges of the path and I showed these to her and we started picking them for Mummy. When she was well started I moved a little way off and when she noticed I had gone I told her to bring me the basket to put mine in and so we went on getting a little further apart each time. At last I actually turned a corner so that I was just out of sight. This time I called to her before she noticed that I had gone and told her to come and find me. She turned up certainly with rather an anxious face but no crying and we were soon running about all over the kitchen garden without the least fear. Presently we started climbing ladders and looking over the garden wall into the flower garden. Sometimes we made short excursions through a little green gate into the wood and were very happy, but one day we nearly came to grief.

We were near the greenhouse and I was just out of her sight although I could see her and a great big bumble bee came flying as only bumble bees can, straight at her face and then turned off just in time—her mouth opened and her hands went up with fists doubled as they always did in one of her screaming fits, but before she could give more than one shriek I had taken her hands and was holding them to her side and told her to *stop that noise at once*. She was so surprised that she shut her mouth and opened her eyes and only saw me and no bumble bee. Then I told her that the poor little bee had got into the greenhouse and was afraid it was a trap and he would never be able to get out and go home, but he had just suddenly found the door and was in such a hurry for fear it would shut that he had buzzed out and nearly bumped into her, but had just managed to buzz round and now he was so happy he could go home and that there was nothing for her to cry about and she did not.

After that on several occasions when the poor baby felt she must scream, she came running up to me to be stopped, which I thought showed a lot of sense. After that we took longer excursions into the fields to the 'Wishing Well', which was a little spring with a stream from it and we dabbled in it and gradually got used to the idea of running water. Then we tried the river and presently played in the boat tied up and a little later went for a row with her to steer and the getting in and out were great feats of skill on her part as I only showed her how, I never lifted or pulled her, she climbed all by herself.

Her father had been away most of the fortnight when all this was going on and I don't think I have ever seen a man more surprised and delighted than he was in the change in the child. She ran down the path all by herself to meet him and went off dancing down the fields with him, a thing that had never happened at all before. Nurse would have had to come too to hold her hand or carry her and probably she would have been brought back at the first stile for fear of exciting or frightening her. Now she was a companion he could take all round the place with him and she loved to go.

There does not seem to be much of my baby in this story, but he came at last and all was well and I went, having been there thirteen weeks, but before I went another thing happened. I used to be driven into Kilkenny on Sundays to church until the baby arrived, then I had not time to spare, but one Sunday the Scottish groom was driving me out in the pony trap after the service, when just as we were passing a row of very poor little cottages where some boys were playing in the road, a little lad of about 12 jumped backwards suddenly against the trap and was knocked down.

Of course we stopped at once and I jumped out to see how much hurt he was. I picked him up and found his leg was broken so I carried him to the trap and said we would take him straight back to Kilkenny to the Hospital. His mother was still in bed and not sufficiently recovered from the drink she had had last night to be able to come with us. The poor little chap was simply filthy and crawling with vermin but luckily he kept them all to himself in spite of my having him on my knee all the way so that I could hold his leg still, as we had nothing that would do for a splint handy and we did not want to have to take him in to his own home, which was one of the dirtiest of the row of cottages. We handed him over to a very adequate looking nurse and doctor and explained where he came from saying that the mother would arrive when she was able. On the way home we met her, hair streaming behind her, no shoes or stockings and dress half undone. She was shouting as she ran and waving her hands over her head, so we stopped and I told her the boy would be quite all right in hospital and she need not worry about him and on we went.

After that, if ever the groom drove into Kilkenny by himself, the mother and other children all ran out and threw stones at him, but if I happened to be in the trap they ran out just the same, but only bobbed and waved their hands smilingly to me, so as often as possible I used to be taken along as a mascot to protect the groom when he had to go into the Town as there was no way of avoiding that little row of cottages.

One day some time later I met the mother coming up to the house and asked her what was wrong as she seemed in some distress. She at once poured out a long story of how they had sent her Joey back from hospital with a terrible skin disease on his leg which they had given him there and now what was the gentleman going to do about compensation for *that*. So far he had only paid them anything because of the broken leg and now that was quite well—praise be! What would himself be doing by reason of the terrible trouble they would be having with a boy at home and nobody to look after the same. He would never be better at all from the disease of the skin of his leg that they had given him in hospital and then sent him home a cripple for life. I told her I was sure the boy would not be a cripple for life and that the Hospital certainly had not given him any skin disease—if he had one it was at home that he would have got it by reason of the dirt in her house. If he had a sore on his leg she better see that it was kept quite clean and it would soon heal up as he was a healthy boy and she had no call on anybody to do more for her than had already been done, so she better go home. However, she would go on up to the house to see if she could get anything. I was there in all 13 weeks and left everybody progressing favourably.

Case 34

About three weeks later I was sent for to see Matron—she wished to see me about a case I was to go to on the following day. I was to wear mufti as the patient did not want it to be known that there was a nurse in the house, but I was to give massage if necessary and take her out walking etc. What was supposed to be the matter with the lady Matron did not know, but she believed my chief duty was to try and raise my patient's 'moral tone'!! and I was to stay there for three months.

I was told that I would need strong boots for country walks and just a blouse or something of that sort to change into in the evenings—no real evening dress as I would dine alone if they had company or with the governess in the schoolroom if she was there and also every weekend, when the husband was home, Matron added that I would need tack and that the patient had asked for another nurse who was not available.

It was a very large house, some miles out of Newmarket, quite in the country and only the tiniest village anywhere within walking distance. Besides owning a large piece of land they rented all the shooting in the district. It was delightfully situated with woods and ponds, large stretches of pasture and a little plough land. They bred enormous numbers of pheasants, but also to some extent encouraged the fox as they liked to have a meet at the house once or twice a year and like to think the Hunt could rely on them for a certain draw and a good run when they came. The house, although oldish, was very spacious and had been modernised and done up without any regard to expense and the same with the garden.

I arrived and was shown in—Mrs. T was in the hall awaiting my arrival. There she was a large rather coarse, once handsome, woman lounging in a luxurious chair. 'Hay, what is your name—I was not expecting you—I asked for Nurse . . . .' I told her my name and said I was sorry but the nurse she had asked for had not been available, so Matron had sent me instead. I was then told tea was ready and we had a sit down one with the children.

I gradually learned from the governess, nanny and my own observation many things.

1. That this was the second Mrs. T. The original one been a 'lady—a real lady' and very nice.
2. *This* was her 'lady's maid'.
3. The original Mrs. T. had left her husband on her account.
4. She was now dead and her daughter—also 'very nice' had recently come of age and refused to live there any longer, so her father had given her a house elsewhere.
5. She came at Christmas and such like times to stay because she liked her father and was very fond of her half brothers and sisters, but her step-mother she could not abide—they were always quarrelling.

Mrs. T., it seems, was very keen on giving her stepdaughter large doses of aperients, which she resented, saying she did not need them. The final rupture came when the girl discovered that her stepmother was having calomel mixed with her cabbage, her portion being put on her plate at the side table like that of the younger children.

Papa was the head of a very large wholesale grocery firm. A pleasant kindly old bounder with no pretensions whatever. He was generally away from Monday early until late on Friday and as often as not, when he did come home his wife for no reason that he or anybody else could fathom, refused even to speak to him all the time he was at home, or if she did speak was so rude that everybody wished she had not spoken. All that I could really find wrong with Mrs. T was a very swollen head and a considerably over filled tummy and a dirty mind. She began by trying to be an interesting invalid. She would race upstairs and down again, then flop in a chair and send for me to feel her pulse as she thought there must be something wrong her pulse was going so fast and making her pant. I was quite brutal about it and told her anybody could play that trick. She then took to staggering in her walk and wanted to know what that indicated. I told her that if she left her walking stick at home and wore sensible shoes she would soon learn to balance herself without any trouble. When I told her that she would feel less swollen inside and have less flatulence if she ate less and took more exercise, she gave up asking me any more questions about her health and took to talking scandal instead.

A neighbouring clergyman had a woman living in the house—he called her his 'housekeeper' but in these lonely places you know. Mrs. So and So has had the district nurse attending to her ever since July, they call it dropsy, but you know her husband has been dead over two years now and they say last time she was out she looked very suspicious. She bought a special kind of pill they keep and she has been ill ever since—probably has been doing something to herself. And somebody else's daughter—she had to be sent away quite suddenly on a long visit—they say so and so, but you know etc. To all of which I only said 'Oh' or nothing.

Whenever we met a man in our walks we had to stop and talk and before we went on she had forced him one way or another to express admiration for her generosity—for giving £5 towards a piano for the village hall, or inviting the tenants to a meal or subscribing to the village nurse etc.

It is a long time since I wrote in any of these little books and not having the old ones by me I can't remember where I had got to, but I don't think I ever said anything about a certain foreign Countess I went to nurse in the Isle of Wight.

Case 19

My patient was French but spoke English perfectly. She, her little son of about 8 and an Irish lady who acted as governess to the boy and companion to his mother, had come to winter in the Island and meanwhile the Countess' doctor, who was an Italian, had suggested that a 'rest cure' might be a good thing and so a nurse was sent for. I was only given the doctor's address, so when I arrived I took a cab and drove to his house. Of course, he was out and so my box had to be set down in the porch while I waited a little further inside the house. Presently the doctor returned and gave me my patient's name and address and instructions that if carried out in full would last at least 6 if not 8 weeks.

We were not to begin the cure I found on arrival until my patient had 'settled a few matters' the next day and the doctor had been. I found I was expected to sleep in my patient's room, a thing Matron absolutely forbids in case of rest cures, as whatever happened to the patient, the nurse would not get any rest at all under the circumstances. So I had to break it to the patient and other arrangements had to be made.

During the next two days the 'matters' that had to be settled continued and the lady companion came in at intervals, each time with a new story against the doctor, who meantime had been in and explained that nobody but he and the nurse and the landlady were to see the patient for the next 6 weeks, and that she was to be kept on a strict diet. Then the companion began to suggest that the doctor might have evil designs on his patient and then however miserable and uncomfortable she was she would have no means of communicating with anybody, as the nurse and the landlady were *sure* to be in league with him.

Then the patient began to say that six weeks was far too long—that was not what she called a 'rest cure'. A 'rest cure' as she understood it only lasted three or four days and meant that absolute stillness, dark and quiet were provided, which could not be done in this place, so close to the sea, that always made a noise and the road where carts rumbled and with a nurse who was to massage her, it was nonsense and could not be done. Then the doctor and the companion started quarrelling—he said she was only disturbing his patient and she must not come any more, but she said she must, there were things to be settled about the boy and she must have that done before his mother was taken and shut away from him for so long—so she had to be let in once more and while she was there informed the Countess that up at the

119

Hotel, where she stayed, she had heard of a far better place, a regular nursing home specially intended for giving rest cures, but this doctor was not allowed inside the doors. There she could be treated just as she chose and she could see her and the boy whenever she liked—but up there there were stories about this doctor and they never took a patient who was under him as they did not approve of him. He was so clever, oh yes, they allowed that he was clever, but there were other things, wouldn't it be better to leave this doctor and go there. Was it quite safe to shut oneself up with a woman one knew nothing of and a doctor who had such things said of him.

Then she went and talked to the landlady, who was up in arms in a moment, seeing that she was to be done out of a good long let. The landlady went to the doctor and the doctor went for the companion and the companion went to the patient, with the result that in five days the doctor left the house, refusing to come back, the patient quarrelled with the landlady to such an extent that she refused to keep her and the companion went off triumphant with the Countess and all her belongings to the nursing home, where one could be treated as one chose.

I was left alone in an empty room and so thought it best to return to Hospital where my account of the Countess' rest cure was treated with much merriment. I found out afterwards that the nursing home that the Countess was taken to was a rather doubtful place, chiefly used for epileptics who were sent there by rather unscrupulous doctors who pretended that 'rest cures' were the best way of treating that complaint, because they had 'an interest in the home' and found it paid. The Italian doctor was not allowed inside because he had once tried to show up these people, but he was a very clever doctor himself and his practice did not suffer to any extent through the evil speaking of 'those who knew'.

Case 20

The next case I went to was also a 'modified rest cure', but it was modified to such an extent that it turned into a very enjoyable stay at the Beacon Hotel at Hindhead. My patient was an elderly lady who provided me with a bicycle so that I could go and see my friends when she rested in the afternoon and at other times we either went out with a donkey chair or for walks or sat in a sheltered balcony when it was fine enough. We stayed there for about five weeks and then I returned to Hospital leaving my patient much improved.

When I went to the 'Office' I was told that I certainly might take the days off that were due to me and so at once accepted the offer of tickets for the theatre and went off with another nurse.

Case 21

On my return to Hospital about midnight, I found to my surprise that there was a note in my room asking me to go and see Miss Larsen before I went to bed, so off I went. When I got

120

thee I found her sitting on the hearth rug trying to keep both awake and warm. She told me that there was a very special case and that Matron would be very grateful if I would not mind putting off my promised days off to go to it.

It was a Marchioness this time, but she was British, so I felt more hopeful about the result of my efforts. It was not absolutely certain but it was probable that she would have to have an operation. Two nurses were required and we were to leave hospital at 4 a.m. in order to arrive as early next morning as possible. As it was 12 now I thought I had better be off and pack and get what rest I could before starting, but just as I was shutting the door Miss Larsen called me back to know what I thought. Was tariff reform or something else, I forget what, the better. What did I think about them. I said I did not know, that I never did think at that time of night and tried to make off again, but this time she called me back to tell me something about my journey or my patient or when I was to be called and so we went on for nearly an hour. At last about 1 o'clock I resolutely shut the door and refused to come back for any more 'last words'. I thought she might get up at 4 a.m. and tell me then if she was so keen.

By the time I had packed and had a bath there was not much time to go to bed so I lay down ready dressed and dozed until I was called and given some breakfast and off we went. When we arrived about 8 a.m. the household was amazed to see us. They had not expected us until midday and nothing was ready, but they made shift to give us our second breakfast and got our rooms ready as soon as they could.

The patient was quite charming, both to deal with and to look at, and so were all the other members of the family including 'little Mary', the youngest daughter of about 2 years or so. For the first two days and nights there were fomentations hourly whenever the patient was awake and the operation was averted and I returned to Hospital on the fifth day and had, not only the days off that were due to me but two extra ones as a reward for not swearing at Miss Larsen and her tariff reform I suppose.

After my days off I was sent to yet another titled patient, an Earl this time who had a stroke. There was already one nurse there from London—another nurse had been there but was sent away as the patient had taken a dislike to her. When I arrived the patient was just a very little better and could just manage to say two words—'window' and 'water'. Very useful no doubt, but not expressive of *all* his wants. For some time we had a good deal of difficulty with him, but by degrees he got better and by the end of three months he was able to do with one nurse and could almost always make himself understood without much difficulty and nine months later when I returned to him for another three months, it fell to my lot to teach him to read and write as before I had taught him to wash and feed himself.

We also spent a great deal of time in the garden, planning for next year and watching the gardeners' plant and the foresters cut trees which were condemned. We used to go round with the steward in a funny little pony trap to the fields and woods on the stage, but it was often very trying at first as my Earl would try to give his orders himself and as often as not said quite the wrong things which puzzled the men a lot—or else he would lose a word and one had always to be at hand and ready with it so one could never let one's mind stray off the matter in hand, because it was not pleasing to his Lordship to be kept waiting even for a word.

After that came various uneventful cases which carried me on for six months or so until one day I was told that I was to go to a case for Mr. Harry Fenwick. Promptly I thought of Cambridge ward, operations and bladder washes, but when I got to Brown's Hotel, Dover Street, with my box I was told there must be some mistake as there was no room ordered for me and my patient was but there was a message for me to go round and see Mr. Fenwick, so I had to leave my box in the hall and go off.

Case 36

On arriving in the great surgeon's consulting room I was greeting cordially with a hope that I knew all about some special form of massage and bath treatment for heart disease! I was rather taken aback. I had vaguely heard of this special treatment but knew nothing of the methods and said so. 'Oh, never mind as long as you can do massage—just fetch that encyclopaedia over here and we will read it up together'. So we did and the result was not altogether satisfactory as it seemed it would hardly be possible to carry it out in all its details in the Hotel or even in a private house. So we settled to modify the treatment by leaving out the baths and adapting the rest to suit our circumstances and back I went with all my instructions to Brown's Hotel where this time I met my patient—a fairly robust looking man somewhere between 40 and 50.

It was arranged that I should return to Hospital for the night and come to him first thing in the morning for one treatment and then he would let me know what time in the afternoon or evening he would be ready for me. For the rest of the day I would be free to do just as I liked. I was to get my lunch and tea when and where I chose and do something either afternoon or evening, go and see pictures or museums or Earls Court or anything I liked and put it down to him. I was not to go back to hospital and work between times for he wanted me fresh—so I spent a very enjoyable week in Town. As a rule I gave him massage and exercises for an hour from about 9.30 to 10.30 and again an hour somewhere between 6 and 8 p.m. At the end of a week I went down to his home at Camberley. He had a lovely big house and garden and the country outside was also very attractive. At the weekends I was left entirely free as my patient preferred to spend them up in Town seeing his friends and did not need a nurse there so I had a very easy time altogether.

* * * * *

A very long time seems to have passed since I wrote anything in this little book. I have been with many different people in a great many different places and it would take nearly a lifetime even to write a little bit about each, so I must skip and skip, or I will never get anywhere near the present time.

The first skip will be over an old Viscountand an old Earl, both quite interesting in their way, and over several ordinary people.

Case 35

Count P. was a huge and to my mind, absurd object with his pain from over-eating and his blue flannel nightshirt—but he slept most of the night and snored so I did not see much of him.

From there I skip over two babies and a very hot summer in Cambridge to a little villa in Finchley where I was for one week at an operation case with another nurse whose people were Quakers, if she was not herself.

Case 38

The patient was a young married woman and she was to have her operation the following day. Her hair was cut short and was curly and she was wearing her husband's pyjamas having sent all her nightgowns to the wash. Her mother, an elderly Jewess, who kept an 'antique shop' somewhere east of the Bank, had come to keep house while she was ill.

The operation was done early and later in the day the husband went to his work, whatever that might be, and all was quiet in the house until about tea time, when I went in just before going to bed to see if I could help nurse tidy the bed and make the patient comfortable. We had almost finished when we heard the gate click and immediately the patient set up the most appalling squeal, 'O, O, they are hurting me, O' and in burst the husband looking very distressed. He had heard her as he came up the path and had hurried to see what was the matter. This happened every day just as the poor man arrived until he began to look at us with great disfavour and think us dreadfully brutal, as we would never allow that his wife was suffering a great deal—but one day he was too quick for her, the gate clicked as usual and he saw us both standing near the window—there was one squeal and he was in the room to find us still near the window and his wife convulsed with laughter not pain.

A day or two later directly the husband had started off in the morning, 'Mama' said she was going to Earls Court Exhibition for the day and off she went leaving the queer old cook in charge downstairs and us up above. All went very happily until lunch time when we wanted an egg for the patient. I had seen a large basket full, a dozen eggs at least, come to the house the day before but nowhere could we find them. We hunted in every conceivable corner, but they were in none of them. I was determined not to be beaten and began to look in the more or less impossible places and there under the sofa in the drawing room were the eggs.

The patient had one, but Mama was not pleased we had taken it without her permission and she was doing the housekeeping. Next day after a very early lunch she again said she was going out, but she would be in to tea and I being sleepy went to bed early. Tea time came but no Mama and no tea, so nurse went down to see what was happening. The cook she found very drunk and put her to bed. The kitchen fire was out and every cupboard was securely locked and the keys in the pocket of Mama. There were two thin slices of bread and butter on a plate and a feeder full of milk, these for the patient, but there was nothing else to be had and nothing to be done but to wait until Mama came home, which she did very late for supper which, of course, was not ready for her or for anybody else, since the cook was drunk and the cupboards were all locked up. I left poor nurse to another fortnight of it when I left and she says that her chief trials were in the presence of and not in the absence of the family.

Case 49

Another leap over Lords, Ladies and ordinary people and over a year passed. Matron wished me to go to a certain lady living in the country, to give her a little massage and er—'raise her moral tone'. Goodness gracious! what a thing to ask a nurse to do. I was to go in mufti and nobody was to know that I was a nurse. I would not need evening dress, but just a blouse to change into as they would be very quiet, but as it was a three month case and three months would take me over Christmas, I just put one in on the off-chance and to be on the safe side.

When I arrived I was shown into the hall where tea was ready and greeted with a toss of the head and a sniff—'So you've come have you—I was not expecting you'. I said I was sorry if she was disappointed but the choice of coming or not had not been left to me—I soon found that I could hardly move for dogs. Much as I like them as a rule, I found fifteen with little if any 'house training', more than I really cared for. My particular friend among the dogs did not arrive for a week or two after I did, but we fell into each other's arms almost immediately on his arrival. He was a beautiful big Russian poodle and a perfect gentleman—the only real gentleman in the whole house—but unfortunately his mistress was extremely jealous because he preferred my society to hers.

To show her disapproval she would wait until 'Don' and I were sitting quietly together and then she would sweep into the room with a trail of other dogs behind her. There was one in particular who always came—a specially low and evil natured brute—broad chested with a protruding lower jaw and the manners of the lowest type of East End bully. He came first, sniffed and looked round making some disgustingly rude remark. Don would shift uneasily, look the other way and pretend not to have heard—the others would jeer and make some worse remark. Don would bristle with disgust and rage but still remained firmly seated beside me. The other would continue getting more and more filthy in his language and possibly making illusions to nationality and courage until at last Don could stand it no longer and with a snarl would go for the beast. If there were not too many and they were mostly small, I could manage all right by throwing some out of the window and then holding the actual fighters apart until I could get the offender out of the room. My patient always disappeared before I could call on her to do anything. One day it came to a climax. There had been five fights in two days that I had stopped and again they started, this time in the schoolroom.

The four children were there and my patient could not get out so started screaming. The dogs were too many and too heavy for me to manage by myself—I was holding two when two more attacked Don and I put out my foot to ward off an unexpected attack from a third. Poor Don, not expecting that sort of assistance, made a bad shot at his adversary and got my leg by mistake. I called to one of the children to run for the footmen as I could not do anything in such a crowd. One little girl bolted off and soon returned with footmen and buckets of water, which they flung about indiscriminately over most of us and finally peace was restored. My patient collected the remains of her 'dear dogs' and retired to bathe their wounds and I went off to old Nanny in the nursery to see if she had any plaster for me. She was most sympathetic and insisted on bathing my leg and bandaging it up herself. One of the children ran in to see what was going on and soon everybody knew all about the two holes in my leg. When I went down presently to lunch all four children said they were sorry and hoped it would not be bad, but their mother never once enquired if it were much and only eyed me suspiciously when it got near the time we generally went out together, to see if I meant to refuse to go out and for a day or two after I think she was a little afraid I might turn and bite her having contracted hydrophobia.

Don was most abject in his apologies for having made such a mistake and we were firmer friends than ever, but we had no more cause for annoyance from the other dog as his mistress was given to understand that there had been enough of that—the dogs might all eat each other before I would interfere again, though I doubt if I could really have stood by and seen Don attacked by half a dozen or so without going in to help him.

One fallacy held by my patient was *that* she loved *all* animals, no matter what they were and so one day when we were sitting by the fire in the evening I drew her attention to a very fine specimen of a mouse that had come out in an interval when the dogs were all away and was sitting up in the middle of the room washing his face. The effect was marvellous—with one piercing shriek my patient clutched her skirts well above her knees and fled from the room. A few minutes later a trembling voice at the door enquired if the mouse were still there. I said it had run off into some corner alarmed by the noise she had made and now would she not come back as the mouse had gone, but she could not do that under any circumstances until she knew the mouse was really gone or quite dead. I must ring the bell for Frederick (the footman) to come and catch it. I laughed and asked if she thought Frederick was a cat that she wanted him to catch a mouse without a trap, but he was said to have done it before and so was sent for. When he arrived he said he could not do it without dusters and somebody to help, so I volunteered and we had a regular steeple chase round the room after a wretched little mouse. The finish was behind a photograph frame that was leaning against the wall— the mouse got behind and Frederick and I fell suddenly on our knees in front of it, our heads coming in violent contact with each other, but we got the mouse and the lady who loved all animals of every description was able to inhabit her own drawing room again.

My patient's husband had made his money in groceries and was not ashamed to own it—in fact he was still doing it. He was one of those round red faced genial old things whom everybody likes and are best described as 'jolly old bounders'—and at any rate where his wife was concerned he had the patience of a saint. He only came home at the weekends or on special holidays as he still worked hard in Town, but although she saw so little of the poor man she often refused so much as to speak to him from Friday evening until Monday morning. When she did condescend to notice him she was often so rude that I felt inclined to hit her, but I never once saw him out of temper. As soon as the Christmas holidays began, weekend parties were inaugurated and a certain amount of shooting, etc. for the men and we used to walk out and have lunch with them and then sometimes walk or stand with the guns in the afternoon and in the evening I used to retire either to my own sitting room or the schoolroom, but about two days before Christmas my patient announced that she thought it would be so much nicer and more friendly if I would come down and dine and sit with them in the evenings which I agreed to do, thanking my lucky stars that I had two dresses, one evening and the other that could easily be converted into a semi-evening one, in spite of the fact that I was told that it did not matter what I wore—I had no wish to feel a freak.

I chose the semi-evening frock the first night and found it was very much the sort of thing everybody else was wearing. My patient eyed me with surprise but said nothing. The next day her maid came to me saying that on Christmas night the ladies would be wearing evening dress. Her mistress had a very pretty grey one that she was meaning to get rid of and would not be needing—didn't I think that if altered a little . . . '. I thanked the maid very much but said I thought I could manage all right and really preferred my own clothes and so turned up in my own grey frock and an Indian scarf, again looking not very unlike most of the younger members of the party. Again my patient eyed me but this time not in mild surprise, but with fury and disgust that was not at all what she had planned. I neither looked peculiar and out of it nor could she compliment in a loud voice on how well I looked in her clothes.

However the Christmas and shooting parties went off very successfully on the whole and only once was my identity as a nurse proclaimed—it was at dinner and my neighbour was telling some story of the ways of doctors (he was one) and nurses which seemed to me both generally untrue and objectionable, so I told him and the company in general that I was sorry if his story was true of his own hospital, but it certainly was not of most. He demanded to know if I was a nurse in disguise as my knowledge seemed to be too positive to be merely secondhand and I had to own to it, but nobody seemed alarmed or surprised as they had all seen my letters in the general pile in the mornings readdressed in red ink from the hospital.

Cases 50 and 51

After that I went to a very different household in Cambridge. A young man of about 22 or so was to have an operation on his appendix and two nurses were needed. On arrival we were greeted by a very kind sensible looking lady. Everything seemed to have been arranged for our convenience and comfort and everything seemed to run on oiled wheels.

After we had been there for a short time it turned out that ours was not the only patient in the house. At the far end was the youngest son, a little fellow of about 9 with scarlet fever, being nursed by their own old Nanny and between us the middle son, who had got very rundown and was covered with boils, and was having medicated baths. The father too was being inoculated for a cough that he could not get rid of and yet there was no fuss, no commotion and no complaining.

They all recovered from their various troubles and I stayed on an extra week because the scarlet fever boy was to have his tonsils out. Before I left my first patient insisted on my borrowing a short coat and skirt from his mother and going to run with the 'Trinity Beagles' as that was his favourite entertainment. He walked from point to point, not being quite up to the running, but we had a very jolly day and I was not too dreadfully tired and stiff although I was rather out of training for that sort of thing.

Case 53

A little jump from February to April brings me to a smallish house in Crouch End. A little elderly lady had heart trouble. She generally increased her not too generous income by taking in 'paying guests'. At the moment she only had one, also an elderly lady, but what she really liked to have was a young man rather addicted to drink. She felt she had a call to improve them. She also tried to be young and skittish to amuse them, she always ran upstairs and slid down the banisters, but the doctor said she must give that up and stay in bed and have a complete rest for a week or two. Complete rest in bed always includes being washed in a blanket by a nurse, so I began by asking if I could have an extra one for that purpose, but I was told it was cold weather and they were all on the beds, so I asked if I could have a large bath towel and some small ones, thinking to make shift with those. She told me I would find the bath towel in the bathroom, so I went off hopefully expecting to find a linen cupboard but no, there was one not very clean bath towel hanging on the door, so I went to the little maid of all work and asked her if she could get me another.

She was very sorry but that was the only one to be had. I asked when the washing was expected home—it came next day but 'there aint no bath towels there'. It was positively the one and only one so I took it—what the rest of the house did I don't know because I could not get dry on the one little object I had in my room, more like a dinner napkin than a towel. So I wrote to hospital and asked if they would send me my own as I had no fancy for the general one and we borrowed small face towels from a friend down the road so that the doctor could have an occasional clean one if he wanted to wash after examining his patient.

At the end of a fortnight my patient was up and about and sliding down the banisters as usual and I returned to hospital again.

Case 55

Another baby and then off I went to Worcestershire to take the place of an old nurse who was looked on by herself and some others as the 'prima donna' of nurses, but by most of those who worked with her as 'an unholy terror' and by me personally, in spite of some very annoying characteristics as 'the hugest of jokes'.

When I got there I found that I was to overlap with her for about a week, because the case was a difficult one and I was to see how she 'managed'. There was already a second nurse there, but according to the old lady she was not of much account. In fact as far as I could see from the way she was treated she was considered much on a par with the kitchen maid or the gardener, with regard to nursing. For as a rule when there are two at a case it is not considered necessary for a new nurse to come until one or other goes, however 'difficult' the case may be.

I arrived and found the nurse and my patient in what used to be the dining room of a comfortable country house. It was a large room with French windows looking out on the garden, a lawn with large trees and flower beds beyond. The room itself might have been pleasant enough too, but that the 'prima donna of nurses' would not allow anything 'unnecessary' in it. That meant no carpet, nor curtains, no pictures, no ornaments, only three beds, two for the patient and one for a nurse, one small wooden table and two stiff backed wooden chairs and a screen. It was a bare and desolate place presided over by the 'prima donna'. I thought her in those days exactly like the reincarnation of a Chinese idol, not only in looks but I felt sure that if such a thing ever took to nursing it would behave much as she did.

The patient had fractured her spine, quite high up, in a tobogganing accident and was quite paralysed from her chest downwards. There had been an operation and the bones had united but there was very little hope of her ever recovering. She had been nursed by nuns until my Chinese Idol had gone out to Switzerland to fetch her home and they, unfortunately, seem not to have the elementary ideas of cleanliness etc. and so the poor girl was not only very unwashed, but also covered with bed sores—nineteen in all, now some were better, but still there were plenty to be dealt with.

For the whole of that week we three nurses rushed and scrambled and hurried and I began to wonder how on earth one managed when there were only two. We were all always doing something until the 'prima donna' left, then the other nurse and I looked round with a gasp and wondered what on earth we had been up to all the time! We could not find half the things to do and there always seemed plenty of time to do it in. The patient, too, at last had a little time in which she could see her friends and relations without a nurse eternally turning them out or scrubbing the room or her or in some other way making it quite impossible to have any private conversation with them.

During this week it seemed I would have much to learn, but apparently the first and most important thing was that the room must be swept and tidy and everything absolutely ready by 9 a.m. in case the doctor should arrive. This must be an unvarying rule and quite regardless of the comfort of the patient. She was ruthlessly stripped and washed, scrubbed and polished, then the bed was made and the room swept, which was a truly comic performance and I could not think what was happening the first morning when I came in. My idol was violently tearing up a newspaper, stirring it up in a basin of water and then strewing the damp and crumpled bits on the floor. I asked what on earth she was making such a mess for when she seemed in such a hurry to get things tidy. I was told in a superior way that it was a very good tip she had learnt when abroad; it was instead of using tea leaves—was far more economical and just as good, so I subsided with a grin although I did not see how 'more economical' as tea leaves were there anyhow in large quantities and probably presently maids would be saying there were no old papers left to light the fires with and tea leaves would not take their place then.

When I discovered what the Idol was up to I went and fetched a broom which she promptly snatched out of my hand saying we must hurry as the doctor might arrive any time—but broomless I did not see how I could hurry so I asked if I should go and find another broom and start sweeping from the further corner, but I was told that would be no use, I had much better help her by moving the furniture, so as she was then violently banging the legs of a chair, I removed it. She did not wait, however, to sweep where that chair had been but fled to the far side of the room and began hitting the table about the legs. I rushed across and dragged it away, but she was gone to the fire and was belabouring the fender. No sooner had I got there than she was off and at the second chair, then the legs of the bed, anything and anywhere to get away from me so it seemed. I was panting for breath and struggling not to show my amusement too plainly—then I had an inspiration, while she was over by the window hitting the wainscoting, which I could not move, I ran round the room and picked up the remaining bits of paper and burnt them and so finished that entertainment for the day, but not before I had had quite enough of it and the doctor did arrive.

It was a very comic week but tiring and even the patient agreed that although it was amusing to see us and wonder how soon we would collide it was something of a relief not to have quite such a turmoil.

One day during that week I was given a little time to rest or go out, so I went down to the river which was just below the garden, hired a Canadian canoe and went off and thoroughly enjoyed myself. On getting back I told the idol what I had been doing and her wrath immediately began to rise. I had better not let the family know, they would not like it at all, especially by canoe. It was far more unsafe than a boat and she had gone out in a boat one day and when she had got back they had begged her to be careful, not because they were troubled for her sake, but they had said it would be so very awkward for *them* if she had been drowned.

After the Idol had left we settled down to a far more peaceful condition for a time, but unfortunately it was not to last. The poor patient herself became the cause of unrest. Either the injury to her spine or septic absorption began to affect the brain. She had all sorts of delusions and finally at times was quite violent. Before I left there had to be three nurses. Curiously enough, however mad she was I could almost always get her to behave and talk rationally again for a time when I went to her and she hardly ever was any trouble while I was there, but I could not be there day and night and once or twice the other two nurses had rather a bad time of it.

One day as I was on my way to bed (I was on nights by myself and had to ring if I needed help as neither of the other two could be left alone with her for more than a very short time), I heard a curious sound from the patient's room and looked in to find a struggle going on. The patient had developed extraordinary strength in her hands and had one nurse by the throat and the other by the hair and neither could disentangle the other, but she was quite good again as soon as I came and told her it was all right and she must not do it. Once or twice in the night I thought she was going either to bite or try to strangle me when I was leaning over her to do something, but the most she ever did was to pull off my collar and cap—she never did like me to wear them so I left off putting them on when I was with her.

She lived for about four months more after I left, but never regained her mental balance and so it was just as well she did not live any longer poor thing as the strain on her family must have been terrible.

There was a most charming toad there who used to visit me every night and I was so grateful to him for his amusing company that I can't go on to the next case without mentioning him. There was a square hole at the bottom of the French windows and always about one o'clock I would hear a funny little sound and if I watched the square hole something would appear very cautiously and slowly a head was raised and he had a look. If all was well a very large and heavy body would rise slowly until it blocked the opening and inch by inch he would squeeze in. Once in he had to rest a little and look round again. If I shuffled or made a noise he would either retire quite suddenly or else hunch himself up into as small a space as possible and wait. When he was quite sure all was safe he would very carefully raise himself up to his full height, legs well stretched out and his body a good 2 inches off the ground and then he would walk very gingerly and carefully on the tips of his toes round the room.

As I watched him I always thought of Agog and wondered if that was how he did it. Round the room he went until he came to the table where the lamp stood, there he settled down into a more natural and toad like attitude and the fun began. Quantities of flies stupefied by the head of the lamp fell there and there was a continuous tap, tap, as his nose hit the floor in his efforts to catch them. I think he must have been fairly good at it as he did not often stay long even if left quite undisturbed, then off he went, flop, flop, flop—out of his own front door not to be seen again until the following night.

Case 59

It was not very long before I came in contact with the Chinese Idol again. This time it was an operation case and the patient was a great admirer of the Idol's. He it was who started calling her the 'Prima Donna of Nurses'. He could not dream of being ill without her, but she had not been well and so was not to be allowed to lift and so I was to come too and we were to have a third nurse.

The patient was a very notable person in the Hospital world and so was to have everything of the best. Our theatre assistant was to come and arrange one of the rooms as a theatre in a truly professional manner. A real hospital bed was sent and proved to be too short for comfort, so the hospital engineer came and added six inches to its length and an enormous van arrived with all sorts of comforts as well as necessaries. Never before was there such a performance.

The patient's room was stripped, bare boards on the floor, no curtains to the windows and hardly any furniture. An entirely new set of lights of special strength was installed and a great many unnecessary people as well as the physician and surgeon and their special assistants came and went. The operation was done and all went well and the Chinese Idol was in her glory. As soon as the patient was well enough to take an interest in such things, she sat and talked the most appalling scandal that was ever invented. The other nurse and I did all the lifting and running about, but certain things the Idol could not bring herself to leave to us and one of them was the actual washing of the patient.

I could fetch and carry, lift and turn him, but she must actually apply the soap and water, so the first morning I went in just before her and got the water, towels, soap, etc. and arranged them with the basin on a small table beside the bed and then turned my attention to the washing blanket which was by the fire. At that moment the Chinese Idol came in and before I realised what she was up to, she had seized on the table and all that was on it and raced with it round to the other side of the bed. I asked her why she had not asked me to move them if she liked them the other side of the bed and reminded her that she was not supposed to carry heavy things, but she only said she had not time to spare talking.

Next morning remembering that she had wanted the things on the left side of the bed, rather than the right the day before, I put them ready for her in the place she had moved them to, but I had no luck for when I came in having gone into the next room to fetch something, I found she had come in and moved them all again. This time it was something about not being left handed, so I suggested that I should put the things alternately one day one side and one the other and was told not to be silly, but I had no more bother about that, she left them wherever I chose to put them in the future.

The next trouble was dinner napkins. The Chinese Idol was much shocked at all forms of extravagance and one she could not understand was the custom of the house of having a clean dinner napkin every day for each person. This she considered unpardonable, in the first place the laundry bill. If one used dinner napkins at that rate what must that come to! Then the napkins themselves—how bad for them to have to be washed so often, they must wear out with the mere washing rather than with use. Then the numbers one would have to keep in stock, one must allow at least fourteen to each person in the house. It was altogether more than she could bear and she spoke to the patient's wife about it, but remarkable to relate, with no result.

Well there was one thing she could do and she did it without a word to anyone it really affected—she went to the pantry and forbade the footman ever to supply a napkin to any of the nurses again, so that as there were three of us that would make quite a difference. The third nurse and I noticed their absence that day but said nothing thinking it was just an oversight on the part of the footman, but next day when none appeared we remarked on it and then our Idol told us with a touch of self-righteous pride that it was not the footman's idea but hers and we both with one accord told her quite plainly what we thought of her idea.

We had both as it happened been brought up in families where the use of a dinner napkin was considered normal. Also we had come to believe that when one was temporarily in another person's house it was bad policy, if not bad manners, to interfere in their domestic arrangements, and it was best to let people order their houses and spend their money in any way that pleased them so long as it was not actually harmful. The result was that the next day the dinner napkins returned and continued to do so until the end of our stay.

Case 62

It was a little under a year after this that once again I found myself in the same house with the Chinese Idol and with the same patient, who was to have another operation. As before there were to be three nurses and all the preparations were as elaborate as before. We had a different third nurse, but as before I was to help the Idol as she loved me in spite of all I said to her. We got on swimmingly and I really began to believe that she had learnt to mind her own business at last, until one day we were waiting for our dinner to come up and she started to say she was sure there were over working the 'hall boy'. There had been an alteration in the arrangements since we were there before and now it was he who carried up our dinner, as since the war had started the footman had left.

This hall boy, she said, was still growing and therefore could not be strong and he should not be allowed to carry up such heavy trays and she must speak about it. At that moment the unfortunate boy came in with a tray of silver and plates etc. and started to lay the table, at which she turned on him. 'Now George haven't I told you not to carry so much on the tray at a time. Look at all those plates—take them away—take them down again—take them downstairs—we can't possibly need all those for two people'. 'Sorry nurse but couldn't I just put them in the cupboard if there are too many and they will do for cold next time then I'd not have to carry them down and up again'. At that moment he looked appealingly at me and I nodded 'Yes, pop them in the cupboard' and he did and went off in a hurry to fetch the food.

Next time he came into the room he brought in one tray having left the second just outside and the moment he appeared the Idol began again. 'What are all those things for? I am sure you have brought up ever so much more than we want—you can take that away I don't want any soup and what is that? I will take a little fish and that now—you can take all the rest away—vegetables? You may leave those now—take the rest away'. The boy looked at me piteously. What was he to do. I saw on the other tray a sweet the Chinese Idol was very partial to and promptly nodded to the boy and said 'that's all right, do as nurse says and take all the rest away' and off he went and we went on with our meal. We ate up our fish and something else and then the Idol looked round. 'Where is the sweet and what was it'. 'It was so and so, you sent it away you know, you told the boy to take everything else away and he did'. 'Oh, dear, I am so sorry. I will run and fetch it myself for you for a penance'. 'Oh, no you don't, you just go without as a penance, because I don't want any myself'—and she did.

Case 63

My next case was an elderly lady who lived in Finchley and had an appendix. It was a fair sized house with a billiard room and two bathrooms and the rest in proportion. The patient's husband was in some kind of business to do with publishing music and was very seldom at home, but there was a married daughter and her little girl staying in the house. When I arrived I was taken into the dining room, it was the beginning of the week and a few days after Christmas and about three in the afternoon. On the dining table were the remains of a meal, a filthy cloth and all the food tumbled about anyhow. The remains of the turkey looked as if it had been gnawed and mixed up with it all was a pile of soiled linen.

Upstairs everything was in a state of muddle and grime. The patient was a poor frail little old lady with hands worn with much work, but nobody else seemed to do any as far as one could judge from appearances. The second nurse came later and we prepared for the operation which was to be next morning. Every plate, cup and spoon that came up for the patient was filthy, bits of the last meal, if not the one before that, adhered to everything and I began to wonder how long we would be able to bear it. Things coming upstairs one could wash oneself, but there were one's own meals downstairs with the family and one could not very well insist on washing one's own things before beginning.

During the preparations that first evening, nurse told me she had just that day had eight teeth out and her mouth was very sore so that settled one point, she must be on night duty and have her meals upstairs so that anything she put in her mouth could be washed first, as I had no wish for her to get a septic mouth from putting dirty things into it. The next question was where were we to sleep. The only spare spot, after that first night, would be the billiard room as there were some more relations coming to stay after the operation was over. So the billiard room it had to be and the daughter said she would see to its being made ready for us to use as a bedroom. She would see to everything so that nurse could sleep there that very afternoon.

As usual we were on duty from 1 until 1 and when I went up to call nurse at about 12.30 a.m. I found what looked for all the world like a small white cocoon lying out on the floor. Really it was the narrowest of narrow camp beds with nurse in it. The little bed looked very forlorn all alone there stuck out away from the wall in a large open space that had been cleared by pushing two or three big easy chairs down to the further end of the room. That was all the 'getting ready' that had been done—no attempt at a dressing table or wash stand—not even a jug and basin on the floor, nothing but a very minute bed and its bedclothes, one pillow case and one set of sheets. However we survived and I brought up a few necessities that were for the time being not necessary to the patient, from her room.

Next day I found a screen and put it round the bed and I unearthed quite a useful quantity of bedroom crockery and a looking glass. I was told that the family always washed in the bathroom and that was why they had not thought crockery necessary in a nurses' bedroom. However, as the family always washed in the bathroom and dressed running about the passages, I preferred not to and continued to use the basin I had acquired up in the billiard room.

There were two bathrooms however and I wondered if a bath might not be possible some time of day or night and went to inspect. The inspection did not take long, both baths were so utterly filthy that I could not imagine that they were ever used for anything but emptying slops into. I did not feel that it was possible to take my clothes off in the bathroom, let alone get into the bath, so next day I made my sponge etc. up into a nice tidy parcel and went out for a walk. About two miles away there was a bath that I knew in the house of an old patient of mine, there I knew I could go whenever I felt a desire to be clean.

I only spent a fortnight at that case but it was long enough and I was sorry for poor nurse when I left and she had to come down to meals and face the filthy tablecloth and crockery and still filthier spoons and forks.

Case 67

Two or three more cases and then down to Devonshire to one of my many baby cases. My patient's husband had been Commander on one of the 'Clan' Line, which was a converted patrol boat, but about six weeks before there had been a most dreadful storm as the patrol had been going up the north west coast of Scotland. One of the other boats had picked up a broken wireless message from the 'Clan' and tried to get in touch again; failing to herself, she tried the other boats. They answered all right and then followed a search. The whole patrol beat up and down that area for hours, first in search of a ship and then of wreckage or survivors, but no sign of anything could they find and not until about three months later was any vestige of the 'Clan' discovered. Then, near Iceland, a small square of wood with the 'Clan' crest nearly rubbed off and a splinter of wood with part of its name painted on it, were picked up in the sea. They were evidently all that remained of one of the ship's boats and all that was ever discovered to tell of the fate of the 'Clan' and her entire crew.

I was surprised at being sent for quite so soon as it was a good three weeks earlier than I had been asked for, but luckily I was free and so down I went. When I got down there my patient hoped it had not been inconvenient for me to come so much earlier, but her mother, on hearing of her husband's death, had come over from Spain to be with her and then they had got news of her only brother's death in the Dardanelles and her mother had been so dreadfully upset that she simply could not bear to be in the house with her alone any longer. She cried all day long and talked continually of nothing else, never leaving her for a moment to herself and she felt that for the baby's sake she *must* be protected from her mother. Her mother, it seemed, had never been very fond of her, but she had been absolutely devoted to the son and now was never tired of telling her that now she had nothing left worth living for, since her son was dead. She cared for nothing and her daughter was no sort of use to her. I thought what a mistake for her ever to have left Spain and her husband who was old and not up to travelling just then, but there she was and it was no use wishing she was not, so I settled down to the protecting of the daughter.

I was told all sorts of stories of how hysterical the daughter had been when her two other babies were born and how the doctor had feared for her reason and how utterly unmanageable she had been with everyone except her husband and how terribly she would behave now that he was dead, but somehow I felt pretty sure that if I and the doctor had her to ourselves there would not be so very much trouble so I hoped and hoped that 'granny' would be sound asleep in bed when baby did turn up.

I was a little nervous, however, as the doctor lived 30 miles away and we had no telephone but had to send a man about three miles on a bicycle to the nearest public call office when we wanted him. I saw the doctor one day soon after I arrived and he said that if I allowed him an hour from the time the message was sent from the office he would be sure to arrive, but when the time did come and I sent a message I thought I would not run it as fine as all that, so I gave the man an hour to do his three miles, an hour for the doctor and then another hour as nearly as I could calculate and still the doctor never came.

It was the middle of the night, much to my relief, and Granny slept sound for all her grief. At 4 a.m. I sent the man off to telephone as we had been able to make special arrangements so as to be able to call up the doctor in the night if necessary. By 5 a.m. he was back saying the doctor had answered himself and would be over in an hour's time. 6 a.m. came and no doctor, 6.30 and still no sign of him, 7 came, 10 past and the baby came in triumphant with a good half hour to spare. When the doctor came, baby and mother had almost settled down to the monotony of ordinary life and nobody except the people I had actually wakened had been any the wiser and 'Granny' had the news of the arrival of a fine new grandson brought in with her early morning tea. Neither she nor her daughter had so far heard any particulars about the son's death, but both were daily expecting letters from his and their various friends and under the circumstances I thought it would be best, if there were any unpleasant or harrowing details, that my patient should not have the letters until she was a little stronger. On the other hand if there was anything that could be of any comfort to her the sooner she heard the better, so I explained this to 'Granny' and asked her if she would just look through all my patient's letters before she had them and keep back any she thought would be specially distressing.

The third day after the arrival of a baby is almost invariably a trying one. That is the day on which castor oil appears on the scene and every other trying accompaniment and if ever anything does go wrong that is the day it will choose, aches and pains appear and even abject misery, and this patient was no exception to the rule, she was very miserable and so I noticed was 'Granny' lending signs of sympathy perhaps I thought. Presently as usual she went in to read her letters carrying a bundle, some opened and others not, and I left them while I attended to other things. When I returned 'Granny' departed mopping her eyes and my patient seemed more miserable and uncomfortable than ever, but said nothing and the day went on through all its discomforts.

The milk came with a tremendous rush and made her breasts almost unbearable, they were so hard and distended by night that I expected to be kept up fomenting them until morning, but by about 10.30 I had got her a little more comfortable and was just going off to get a bath when she suddenly asked me if her mother had said anything to me about any of her letters, because when she had come in that morning she had in her hand an open letter on the ship's paper and in the writing of her brother's greatest friend on board ship and there was time enough now for them to be hearing from them about his death. She was afraid that her mother had not even read her bits of the letter; that the details must have been too dreadful and that he must have suffered a great deal.

'Granny' had not mentioned a word to me but I thought it was high time I knew something mor about the matter, so I went off to her room and routed her up and asked her if she could tell me what was in the letter or let me read it so that I could judge for myself which was worse, knowing or not knowing, as I could see no reason for trusting to her intelligence after the lack she had shown in taking the letter into the room in the morning if she had not meant to read it. She read it to me—there was nothing in it, since the fact of his death was no fresh news that could possibly be anything but a comfort. His popularity, his keenness, his bravery, his quick and painless death, his contentment that his job was done and that even if he had lived he could not have improved on the working of his gun and crew. I had that old lady out of bed and into my patient's bedroom in next to no time, letter in hand and when she went back my patient was a different creature. Not entirely comfortable I own, but what did that matter compared with the mental distress she had been relieved from.

A few days later a message came in from next door, could we let the district nurse have various things as she was there with the farmer's wife whose baby was coming and she had got nothing ready, it being her first one and she had not known and never thought of asking. I sent in everything she asked for and some hours later went to enquire how things were getting on. It seemed they were simply not getting on and when next morning came and the report was still much the same I suggested that perhaps a doctor might be of some use. At last he was sent for and after a great deal of trouble and more time the baby turned up—not a very large one but quite healthy, although the poor mother was quite knocked up after 2 days and a night of really hard work. The district nurse, not having been engaged beforehand, said she could not possibly come in and see to her every day and the doctor, being very overworked as he was doing two partners' work as well as his own, the others being away at the War, was afraid he would not be able to get round that way again for three or four days at any rate and asked if I would mind just looking in now and then to see that the old granny, who was being sent for, understood what she was to do and that the patient was getting on all right. As a matter of fact both baby and mother got on splendidly and when I left my case next door, my accidental patient rushed out of her house as I drove past and presented me with a large jam pot full of the most delicious Devonshire cream she had made from her own cows and I carried the pot triumphantly back to Town on my knee.

Case 68 June 2nd 1915

After this case I had days off and my holiday and when I returned heard that I was already booked to go to a friend of the Chairman. He had not met him for a long time and was afraid he had fallen on bad times and into bad ways, but I was to do what I could and put up with as much as possible. My destination was some three miles out of a village in Ayrshire. The house had once been a 'shooting box' and was reached by a field track about half a mile in length which crossed the railway by a small bridge just outside the front gate. At the back of the house was an over grown garden which sloped away rapidly to the lake or rather a series of lakes all surrounded by bogs and in the distance were the mountains. The whole placed looked uncared for and the sound of a harsh and rancorous voice scolding did not lend cheerfulness to the scene.

My patient was a man of about 70, perhaps rather less, but illness had aged him so that one could hardly guess his age with any feeling of certainty. He was recovering from an attack of influenza but seemed unable to make the needful effort toward perfect recovery and he was also addicted to morphia. He was a kind and patient man by nature but as was natural with his complaint he was often very depressed. The doctor said that in his present state of health it was quite impossible to try to decrease the morphia habit and the most I could possibly do was to prevent it from getting any worse.

It was a queer rambling house and there was one servant called the cook, but her mistress said she was far too dirty to be allowed to do any cooking so she did it. The first time I saw her at it I felt I could never eat anything she had had dealings with again. I preferred the dirty cook, who after all was only black with black lead and smuts whereas her mistress drank strong whiskey and soda and smoked cigarettes all the time she was cooking and dropped the ash in the puddings and bread and more than once I saw her feed her favourite dog with the spoon she was using and then go on stirring the pudding without even wiping the spoon.

The dog was a very special black and white setter and suffered from consumption and if ever he went out for a day's shooting had to be forcibly fed with Brands Essence and egg beaten up with brandy in the middle of the day as he got so exhausted he would not eat his proper food! But the husband got none of this care—he could have any old thing made any old way.

I had not been in the house long before I found that the pony was really the prime favourite and if anything happened to it there would be greater distress than if any other member of the establishment was in trouble. In fact, Mrs. C told me quite frankly that she did not care one bit who died so long as the pony remained in good health. She also told me that she intended to go and live in Richmond taking the pony with her when her husband died and she had already bought all her mourning.

Unfortunately for her, after three months of ordinary care and attention I left her husband in better health than he had been in for years. After I had been there for a little time I began to wonder what Mrs. C could possibly do in the night. I always heard such a noise going on in her room. One day I asked her if she was moving furniture or what but she denied having made any noise. She had two large dogs and two small ones sleeping in her room and a night or two after I had asked, the large retriever came and burst into my room in the small hours sniffing round the walls as if looking for something, then came and looked at me rather puzzled and then went out. This happened two or three nights running, the dog getting quite excited if it could not get in. At last I expostulated with Mrs. C and told her she must keep her dogs out of my room, to which she replied that the dog heard me moving things in the night and came to see what was the matter, but I knew that until the dog woke me and I got up to turn her out, all was quiet in my room.

The morning after that I was sitting quietly in my room when I became aware of a horse going at a tremendous pace along the road, it hardly slackened as it turned into the field track and one heard the rattle of a two wheeled trap or dog cart behind it. It raced at breakneck speed across the field. I heard the hollow rumble as it went over the bridge and all four dogs rushed out towards the gate barking. The horse and trap got on the rather coarse shingly gravel and drew up with a jerk at the front door, all the stones scattering as if the horse had nearly sat on its haunches with the suddenness of its pull up. I looked out to see whoever could be arriving in such a hurry and there was nothing there, only the four dogs coming quietly back from the gate with their tails between their legs and looking very sheepish as if trying to say 'we are sorry we were so silly'. I asked Mrs. C if she had seen or heard anything of it and she said no, but that she often heard the noises I complained of in the night. She always heard them in my room, they were never in the same room with the person who heard them. She had been told that there was a ghost connected with the house, other people had heard my horse and trap, but she had never been able to get any explanation nor hear the story connected with it. The local people were afraid to speak of it and she had only lived there a few years herself, so I never got to know any more about my ghostly horse and cart. The flowers in the bog, the birds and the beasts on the hills and in the woods around, were fascinating but that is more than I could say for the human inhabitants with the exception of the keeper and his family. They were thoroughly nice simple country people and when an addition to the family turned up all in a hurry one morning and I found mother and baby sitting on the kitchen floor together all by themselves, I was delighted to go and put them to rights and send for 'granny' to look after them.

After a stay of about ten weeks I returned south—Weybridge and Bournemouth saw me.

Case 71

About Christmas time I was back in London nursing an operation case. The patient was a lady well known in the scholastic world and a friend of hers had offered to take her and me in for the operation. The friend's house was a small one, so the drawing room was given up to the patient for the operation and as a bedroom afterwards. It was a little inconvenient, however, we did manage pretty well and the only person who seemed really uncomfortable was the owner of the house who seemed to think there was some ban against sitting in the same room with me while I had my meals and used to banish herself into the bathroom.

One day a nephew came home from the war and came in to see his Aunt. The war had been going on for some time by that time and there had been a good many very vivid descriptions of the hardships the soldiers had to put up with. The Aunt asked about some battle the boy had been in and he said in a reassuring way that they had been able to take cover and were perfectly safe in the shelter of a gravel pit and the water was only up to their knees, where at that the poor Aunt was horror stricken. Did he get his feet wet? She hoped he had changed his socks at once. The poor boy looked at me and said no more. What could he say if she had not taken in more than that.

Case 72

This was a confinement case in London. All went well and the baby arrived and the patient's mother, who was an Austrian by birth, was extremely anxious to make herself useful. To take the baby into the next room, to come in and help with the patient herself and dressed herself up in a large apron for the purpose. In fact, she longed to do anything except keep out of our way, which was what we really wanted her to do. However, she was the mother and probably anxious so we bore her importunity, though without giving in to her requests. When all was over she went off to her home not so very far away and we saw no more of her until the next day when she came along in the afternoon to see if she could sit with my patient, as before dressed up in a large overall. I thanked her very much and said she could go in and see her and I would just run along to the post office as there were some important things my patient wanted to have sent which her husband had forgotten to take when he went in the morning. I was away about half an hour in all and everything was all right when I returned.

On the third day there were the usual performances with castor oil etc., but by about 3 p.m. my patient seemed quite comfortable and the baby was quiet so I again accepted the offer of half an hour's run. On my return Granny met me in great excitement—as soon as I had gone my patient had needed attention, but Granny had nobly risen to the occasion and all was well so I thought no more about it and was quite unprepared, when I went in, for being sent for by Matron. She wanted to know what the doctor meant in his report—could I give an explanation? It was that I had neglected my patient and had left her immediately after confinement when she was in great danger of haemorrhaging and he understood that the extra £1. 1s. 0d. paid to the Hospital by maternity patients was to ensure the patient's not being left after I had seen him.

Granny's and my quarrel had been over the treatment of the baby and she had even gone so far as to accuse me of trying to kill it and that I, like every other nurse, was trying to prevent the mother feeding it herself, because it was less trouble to have baby on bottles. It was no use arguing so I just told her that I was not such a fool and if she was not one she would realise that killing babies was not good for the reputation of a maternity nurse. However, though the baby seemed perfectly happy and comfortable it was not growing and I could not think why, it seemed so contented after its food that one could not think that it did not agree with it, or that it was being starved. But we thought it might be worthwhile to get the mother's milk analysed and Granny resented our thinking it possible there might be some fault in anything to do with her daughter.

When the result of the analysis came back we found that there was about twice as much of all the solids as there should be so poor baby was only having half rations of water, so the

139

trouble was easily set right by giving him a drink of water after each meal and from that moment he began to swell almost visibly. Matron was quite satisfied that I had not really done anything very dreadful and I heard no more of Granny or the doctor, but I once met the baby in the park with his Nanny and he looked very well although ugly!

Case 73

Again I was with the very notable person who could not be ill without my Chinese Idol, but she was totally unavailable, having gone as Matron in some Convalescent Hospital for soldiers, so we had to get on without her. The patient had had an accident and was knocked over by a lorry. He was picked up unconscious and taken to the small local hospital, nobody knowing in the least who he was as they could not find anything about him at first to identify him by. At last someone in hunting over his clothes found a small bit of tape sewn on his coat, waistcoat, trousers and tie with 'grey' written on it—for a time he became Mr. Grey, but not for long—what the grey really meant was that he wore this particular black coat, coloured waistcoat and tie with his grey striped trousers. In some other combination of clothes he would have had to be Mr. Brown or Blue.

Soon our great man began to babble of the London Hospital and so they sent there to see if someone from the Hospital could come over and identify him and Mr. Morris, our Secretary that was and now House Governor, went and was able to give him his real name. Not only did the Secretary recognise the patient, but the patient, the Secretary. News was sent to his wife and nurses from the Hospital turned up and I was among their number—although I had started off on my days off, I was recalled. When I arrived I was taken into the small ward that had been emptied for his use. The patient seemed to know at once that I was a newcomer as he asked me at once where I was trained. He had asked his wife the same question on her arrival and she knowing what answer would be acceptable had promptly answered 'Oh the London Hospital of course' and he had been quite satisfied. I too was trained at 'The London' but that was not enough he wanted my name—I told him 'Hart' and he at once replied 'Not Wilby Hart' and I said 'yes' but he would not have it—Nurse Wilby Hart was a great tall woman and all the nurses here were little short women; so I told him to pull up the black thing he had covered his eyes with and have a look if he did not believe it, which he did and at once exclaimed 'why so you are' and after that he always knew me even if he did not recognise other people.

It took four of us, two on day and two on night, to look after him as he could not be left for one moment or he would have been out of bed or doing something he should not and the hospital had not staff enough even to relieve us for meals let alone fetch and carry for us. At last after about six weeks he was considered well enough to be taken to the hire house they had in Town and there we stayed until he was well enough to be motored down to his own house in the country and there it was that he began to be really troublesome, as he was not supposed to do any business or write letters even then and he was beginning to feel well enough to do things. He used to surreptitiously get up when he had promised to lie down and rest and write letters and then get one of the servants to go and post them and his poor wife would be greatly puzzled by letters arriving a few days later accepting invitations to come down and talk over business matters or answering questions she knew nothing about.

Cutting wood and feeding golden pheasants were the two great pastimes. A great storm had rushed across England and had uprooted numbers of huge trees a few days before we came down to the country so there was plenty of cutting up for us to do.

Case 74

From there I went on to a nice child of about 16 who was to have her tonsils out. We had a very happy time together and made great friends although I was only there for quite a short time. We had quite a number of mutual acquaintances as funnily enough she was still at school at Lingholt, Hindhead, where I had been teaching for about three years before I started nursing. Three years later we met again when she became the mother of one of the illest babies I ever had on the Private Staff.

Case 75

My 75th case was an operation. My patient, an only daughter of about 30, had an enlarged thyroid which was getting troublesome and so was to be operated on. Mr. Furnavel was coming down to do it, her own doctor assisting and an old 'dug-out' friend of the family was to give the anaesthetic. The patient was under and the first incision made when the anaesthetist, fearing to keep the patient too deeply under, let her come round a little—she started to vomit and before we knew what he was up to he had put his dirty unscrubbed old fingers right in the wound in a vain effort to prevent the vomit from running down her neck. But our luck was in that day and there were no ill effects but we trembled at the time, and on and off for several days, until we were quite sure the wound was healing 'by first intention'.

I was there in the Springtime and there were some beautiful woods not very far off and a wonderful variety of wild flowers. Bee, fly and bird's nest orchids, besides most of the common kinds, herb Paris too and cowslips, forget-me-nots and bluebells in any quantity. I used to come in with large bunches of all sorts of wild flowers, much to my patient's amazement. She could not think where they could come from as she had never seen them although she had lived in the neighbourhood for years and thought she knew the country well—but I don't think she had ever been off the road, except when she went on a tennis court or croquet lawn, which she was allowed to do if Mother came too. Mother was one of those people who are very jealous, she could not bear her daughter to have intimate friends even of her own sex, also she was very middle class, but had not been so long and was in consequence very keen on always doing the correct thing. Poor Doris had been made to leave two tennis clubs because of some real or imagined slight which the other members had offered to Mother, who had insisted on coming and joining as a playing member and now there were no more clubs in the neighbourhood and very few friends and acquaintances, as Mother would not quarrel, but 'took umbrage' at them all.

After this a great gap occurs which may be filled in one day. My old 'case book' not being at hand I start again with number 118.

Case 118 **November 29th 1921**

Sir S.L. When I went to him he was recovering from a severe operation which he had had in a nursing home. He was now returning to his flat and needed to be fitted with a belt etc. and generally set in the way of managing for himself again. I was with him about a month and I hoped he would be interesting. He was very keen on Shakespeare and the 'Old Vic' and was working hard to get money and support for it, but I soon found that it was not so much Shakespeare and the 'Old Vic' that he was interested in as his own views on and remarks about them that he was keen on and how much he had personally done and written on the subject, which quite soon became completely boring, to me at any rate.

Case 119 **December 30th 1921**

My next patient was a lady who kept a wholesale outfitting store for women and children. She had a great many girls working under her, not only storing but making garments, somewhere in the City, but she lived out at Boreham Wood. Hertfordshire is a great place for Gipsy encampments and I made the acquaintance of several families while I was there. Three weeks there saw my patient completely recovered, but in about another three weeks time I found myself in Herts again among the Gipsy encampments, but not quite the same district.

Case 120 **February 11th 1922**

This time I was between Goffs Oak and Cheshunt, nursing what we knew to be a hopeless case from the start. Sir Hugh Rigby came down and operated—not because there was any hope of recovery, but just to ease the patient for the time she had to live.

The old husband, two grown up sons, who had fought in the war, and a daughter who had worked indefatigably in the district, were really rather fine in their impassive kind of way. Never once in their trouble, even on the day the mother died, forgetting the courtesy due to two visitors, strangers in the house, the nurses.

The mother, a German by birth and I think sympathy had seen her two sons in the Army fighting against their own relations, to whom she at any rate was devoted, and their one anxiety now she was dying was to try to get her favourite sister over to see her before she died. They just succeeded.

Most houses at this point—1922—were absolutely devoid of one thing at any rate. If one asked for old linen to tear up for use it was unobtainable, everyone had given all they had, not only of the oldest, but all that was not actually in use, to the hospitals for swabs and bandages etc. We asked here hardly expecting to get anything—the one sign of Germanic sympathy—a cupboard was unlocked and found to be stacked crammed full to overflowing with old soft sheets and towels, pillow and bolster slips, far to worn to be of any use but for swabs and dressings, that must have been stored away for years and not a piece given away. Her linen had been too sacredly precious.

We were about two miles from the village and one day I walked into Cheshunt to post a large parcel of sprouting chestnuts to be grown by various people in Hospital. When I arrived I found it was early closing and the post office was shut. I was just turning away very much annoyed because the parcel was heavy and I had no wish to carry it home again and back the next day, when I heard somebody call me. I turned and saw a pleasant face smiling at me from the other side of the road, the owner a middle-aged man with a rosy face and grey hair was crossing towards me. 'Did you want to get into the post office Nurse?' I assented, saying I wanted to post my parcel, but I was afraid they would not take it now. My friend said he would see what he could do and went round to the back, but found nobody at home so that was no use but he said if I would trust him with it, he would gladly keep my parcel and send it off for me next day, so we went in his shop to weigh it and see how much it would be.

On saying goodbye to me he said if I cared to call on my way to the station when I left he would have a little bunch of flowers ready for me. I did about a week later and the little bunch was forthcoming to such an extent that I had great difficulty in conveying it from the taxi to the train.

Case 121

My next case was a lady said to be suffering from 'Mind Shock' after an accident. She was to have massage and be kept in bed, but absolutely refused to have a nurse sleeping in her flat. She would only have one on condition she never came before 10 a.m. or stayed later than 6 p.m. Luckily my sister lived not very far away and I was able to spend my spare time and sleep there. As time went on my patient found I was quite safe to have about even when her husband was late starting out or happened to come in unexpectedly and when I left finally I had a cordial invitation to come and call any time, but I have not been.

On April 20th I was due for a fortnight's holiday. On the 15th I went out to a case which lasted on until June 3rd. It was a baby case up at Hindhead. The patient had gone there on purpose to be attended by a certain doctor regardless of anything else. The cottage she took had no indoor sanitation and only earth closets when you got there. My only help was a wartime 'land girl'. The rest is better imagined than described.

The Land Girl.

"Is this what potatoes aught
to look like when they are
done do you think?"

Case 126 Jan 2nd 1923 (7 weeks)

Came as rather a shock. I was sent for to Matron's office and told I must get ready at once to go to Sandringham and that tact would be the most essential qualification. Princess Victoria had pneumonia and Miss Fletcher, the late King's nurse, needed help. I was to go as night nurse and do what I could.

Miss Fletcher's vast proportions –

When I arrived Miss Fletcher's vast proportions greeted me and I was sent to bed. I was roused several times during my first afternoon by somebody apparently mistaking my room, bursting in and then going out again. I learned afterwards that it was Queen Alexandra, who was so anxious to see the new night nurse, that she could not be restrained from running into my room. They could not make her understand why I should have to go to bed in the day time, or if I must go to bed in the day why she should not run in whenever she liked and have a look at me. At last she had her way. I was getting up and just succeeded in struggling into the last garment when in she popped. After we had said 'how do you do' she did not worry anymore and only came in at suitable times. I was trained most carefully by Miss Fletcher and for the first two nights I was allowed to do nothing without supervision. On the third morning early Princess Victoria asked if I did not think that we might begin 'before old Betty woke up and get it all over before she came along' and so we did, most successfully.

The room Princess Victoria had was really quite a fair size, but it was all so cluttered up with every conceivable and inconceivable thing that one literally had no room to move. The bed was pushed away in the darkest and most airless corner. There was a shelf running round the wall about four feet up covered with photographs of her relations, a screen at the foot of the bed all three panels covered both sides with more photographs, tables and mantle shelf with more and each one more ugly than the last. Everywhere there were photographs and between innumerable small objects. 6½d. ornaments from Woolworths, cheek by jowl with beautifully carved ivory or carnelian or jade. Her bathroom next door was full of Danish blue and white china on shelves or hanging on the wall and a shelf of books of which I had the run.

The first time I went out, much to my surprise just round the corner I met a London policeman. I greeted him with enthusiasm and I found later there were several of them about, they always came down when any of the family were in residence. It gave one a more comfortable homely feeling to see these men standing about and I wondered if at any time I really felt I could not bear it a moment longer, if I would be able to persuade one of them to help me run away. A foolish idea no doubt, but one that almost always comes to me in a very big house with large grounds. 'Is there a way of escape?'. I must have a good safe line of retreat if I am going to settle down happily and Sandringham is *miles* from the station. Everybody was most kind and everything was done for my comfort. Meals were brought up for me, but Miss Fletcher preferred to go to the servants' hall for hers. The average age of the staff must have been close on 80, some must have been so much over that the few girls cannot have brought it down much and I feel sure there was not a page under 70.

One day the Housekeeper offered to let me see the late Duke of Clarence's rooms. It was she said the anniversary of his death. His bedroom was always kept ready, just as it had been when he used it, but from that day to the anniversary of his funeral each year a fire was lighted and a special silk Union Jack was spread on his bed and a buttonhole placed ready on his dressing table each morning. She said that for some years the bed had always been covered with little nosegays brought and put there by different members of the household, but that Queen Alexander, Miss Charlotte Knowles and one or two of the older members of the household were the only ones that did it now. She pointed out to me some scratches on the window where the Duke had tried to write his name with a diamond and a picture Queen Alexandra had had hung there since his death. It was a photograph of angels welcoming souls into Paradise—I think by Botticelli. In the foreground there is a tuft of leaves, aloes I think, round which the angels and recently arrived souls are dancing. Someone had cut out the head from a small photograph of the Duke of Clarence and had stuck it in the middle of the tuft of aloes! For some reason it made me think of nothing so much as the pictures in 'Shock Headed Peter' where the hare sits behind a bush and shoots at the huntsman and it was all I could do not to roar with laughter. The housemaid confessed to me afterwards that when a bottle of hair lotion began to smell too badly she did throw it away and not replace it, but apart from these few things everything was kept exactly as he had had them, even the old toothbrushes.

I was shown all over the house, each person taking me through his or her own department. The butler showed me the plate, the safe it was kept in was a large room with cupboards with glass fronts all round and a huge case in the middle. The still-room maid showed me the tea cloths, the housekeeper the linen. I saw the horses in the stables, some were so old that they had to be slung at night to save their legs, as Queen Alexander insisted on keeping and using her state horses to the very end. There were some lovely dogs in the kennels. There was a very well kept garden with greenhouses and a charming little dairy where on Sunday in the summer 'Her Majesty' took tea.

The King came down to York Cottage soon after I got there and there were some great shoots. The Dowager Empress of Russia was staying in the House, so was the ex-Queen of Greece, Princess Royal and her daughter Princess Maud. The Queen of Norway came to her own little house not very far away and on Sunday they all came to the little church in the park. The poor King had his work cut out for him as he sat between his Mother and the ex-Queen of Greece (a dear old lady just like an old-fashioned grandmother) and he had to find all the places for both of them and try to prevent his Mother from making too-audible remarks about the congregation, which he found very difficult. not to say impossible!

One day the next week the Duke of York turned up quite unexpectedly and there was a great commotion. He had come to announce his engagement and his father sent him packing off to fetch the young lady to stay for the next weekend. On the 20th January 1923, Miss Elizabeth Bowes-Lyon made her first visit to Sandringham to meet her future 'in-laws'—the Royal Family. On Sunday morning in church the whole Royal Family were in their usual places in the Chancel. I was about halfway down in one of the side aisles when I saw the Duke of York peering down the church, presently his eye fixed on me with a slightly puzzled expression and then a most enormous smile appeared. After church when I was back in my room, I heard a bang on my door and in he came to bring Miss Elizabeth Bowes-Lyon. He had brought her up to see his favourite aunt, Princess Victoria, and had to bring her in to introduce her to his nurse before they went. He had caught sight of the uniform in church and then had suddenly recognised me.

A little later on, they both came and stayed for a week and we saw them about everywhere together. He was undisguisedly triumphant and beamed with pride and pleasure. She too was all smiles and was perfectly charming—quite natural and self possessed although 'Bertie' and Queen Mary were the only two people in all that crowd of future 'in-laws' that she had ever met before.

When Princess Victoria really began to be well enough to get up, we started giving her massage and oxygen instead of letting her get about the house and gradually go out a little, as it was very well known that once Queen Alexandra knew she was up she would think she was quite well enough to be at her beck and call again and she would have no more peace. Then one day came when she was allowed out for a walk and two days later Lord Dawson told her Mother that she must get away to the South of France at once, so she and 'Betty' went off up to Town for a week's shopping before she started and I was left in charge.

A few days before this the Dowager Empress of Russia was taken ill and I had to go and give her a dose and a few other little things and be in attendance while Lord Dawson examined her. He came to the conclusion that it might be something very serious and that she ought to go up to Town and be X-rayed as soon as possible. She had two of the most devoted servants, a Cossack and maid, who never left her. There had been a second Cossack but he had wanted to get married and so had to leave her as she could not afford to pay him wages sufficient to keep a wife on. The others I believe just lived wherever she did and so were kept and occasionally were given presents. The day Lord Dawson examined H.R.H. he hurt her a little and she called out and the maid only just restrained the Cossack in time to prevent him from rushing in to avenge her with his knife.

During the next fortnight I saw quite a lot of the Queen Mother and the Empress Marie. The Princess Xarina and her youngest son came to stay too. Good old Betty had a fortnight's holiday instead of a week's shopping with Princess Victoria. Often when the Empress Marie was bored or had nothing better to do she would send for me and tell me to sit down while she told me stories of her experiences, both before and after the Revolution in Russia. She was firmly convinced that her son was still alive in hiding somewhere and that one day he would turn up again.

She told me of the time when she was imprisoned in one of her own palaces. The sailors came early one morning and pulled her out of bed and ransacked the place. They sat her on a chair in the middle of the room while they stripped the bed and ripped open the mattress, searching for 'incriminating papers'. They were so uneducated that they could not read what they found so everything in handwriting was collected and put in a sack. Even photographs with autographs were taken, but anything printed was left and considered of no interest. All her clothes were pulled out of the drawers and thrown on the floor in their wild search. She meantime was sitting in nothing but her nightgown for about six hours.

The Officer in charge sat in the next room looking over everything the 'Common Sailors' brought him. The door into the passage was left half open and the men all took turns to come and peep and make remarks about her. This made her very angry and she shouted at them to go away, but they would not and she became more angry still and called to the Officer to send them away. He told them to go but they soon came back and at last he had a screen put round her, but they would not let even her maid come to her. She was being kept in another room and they never gave her any tea even though she sat there six hours. The mattresses of the beds were ripped open in case there was anything in them.

Later she was imprisoned in another of her own Palaces and a guard of sailors watched over her, among whom she noticed one of their own men off the Royal Yacht. He was always particularly rude and offensive, cursing whenever she passed and spitting, until one day they met in one of the passages with nobody else within sight. He fell on his knees and kissed her hands and explained that he was only behaving so because he wished to stay and keep an eye on her. She tore off the cross she wore round her neck and gave it to him and he pushed it under his clothes saying he would keep it forever even if it cost him his life. The moment after he was up and cursing her as usual as he heard steps in the distance which might mean the presence of an officer.

She said one night looking out of her window she saw a figure running past in the darkness. A light from one of the windows suddenly flashed out and the figure crouched back into the bushes and she realised that it was one of her daughters with her baby in her arms. She had not been confined in the same palace as she was herself but in one quite nearby. Next day the Princess was missing and there was hue and cry after her but she was not found and it was months later that she was heard of. She had been hidden by one of the gardeners who lived up in the mountains. He passed her off as his own daughter until people began to suspect and then one day he said it would not be safe for her to stay any longer and somehow she was got out of the country.

The poor Empress' description of her own joy on seeing half a loaf of real white bread brought and given to her by the British sailors who came to take her out of Russia would really have been funny if it had not been so pathetic. Her eyes sparkled and she clapped her hands at the thought of her own excitement on seeing it.

Here, the diaries in Tony Shephard's possession are ended, though I feel sure that Nurse Wilby Hart's career was far from over. We would love to hear from anyone who knows of any further diaries in existence, or who can tell us more about this remarkable woman! [JM]